CHURCH ABUSE

By

Sophia Lorraine Wilson

Table of Contents

Introduction

There are wounds that never make it to hospital beds. Wounds that do not bleed on the outside but leave the soul limping quietly. Wounds carried into bedrooms after a Sunday service. Wounds wrapped in silence because you are afraid of being misunderstood, judged, or labelled rebellious. There are wounds caused not by strangers, but from the very place that was meant to protect, nurture, and heal you: The Church.

If you are holding this book, chances are your spirit has been bruised, your trust shaken, or your faith stretched in painful ways. Maybe you've sat in services where the words pierced instead of healed. Maybe you've given your loyalty to leaders who mishandled your vulnerability. Or maybe you've endured environments where manipulation was disguised as spirituality, and control was packaged as obedience. And now, you are tired emotionally, mentally, and spiritually.

This introduction is written for you. For the one who loves God deeply but has been hurt deeply. For the one who walked away, not because you hated the church, but because staying felt like losing yourself. For the one who prayed, cried, forgave, tried again, and still found yourself drowning in guilt, fear, and confusion. For the one who has been carrying questions in silence, wondering if your pain even matters to God. It does, and you do.

You are not imagining the damage. You are not exaggerating the weight. The pain you feel is real, it is valid, and it deserves to be spoken out loud. The church is the body of Christ, but it is also full of humans with flaws, weaknesses, and unresolved wounds. When these wounds are not healed, they spill over into leadership, relationships, and doctrine, creating cycles of abuse that are often ignored or spiritualized away. But pretending something is healthy does not make it healthy. Silence has never cured any wound.

This book opens with a gentle but firm truth: abuse in the church is real, and it must be named. Healing cannot begin where denial is still reigning. There is nothing dishonoring about acknowledging you were hurt. There is nothing unspiritual about admitting that something went wrong. There is nothing rebellious about seeking clarity, safety, or restoration. Too many believers have been conditioned to equate silence with maturity, endurance with spirituality, and suffering with loyalty. Yet the God who sees your tears does not call you to a faith that destroys you internally.

Here, you are invited into a safe space. A space without accusation. A space without pressure to "just move on". A space where your story is not dismissed as exaggeration or immaturity. This is a space where your pain is heard and your heart is honored.

You will not be judged here, nor rushed, nor be minimized. Instead, you will be understood. Because the truth is this: church hurt leaves marks that can follow you for years. It affects how you pray, how you worship, how you trust, how you relate to others, and even how you see God. When the place that taught you about God becomes the place that wounds you, the internal conflict is overwhelming. How do you reconcile loving God with leaving His house? How do you separate divine truth from human manipulation? How do you rebuild when everything inside you feels scattered?

Some people have walked away from the church not because they backslid, but because they were bleeding. Some left not because they were proud, but because they were suffocating. Some did not stop serving God; they just stopped serving what was hurting them. And if that is you, hear this clearly: you are not alone. Many sons and daughters of God around the world are silently nursing injuries from pulpits and pews. Many are wrestling with whether to stay, leave, return, or rebuild. Many are trying to preserve their spiritual sanity while still longing for a place to belong.

This book is not here to shame you; it is here to walk with you. It is here to shine light on what broke you, not to reopen the wound, but to help you see that healing is possible. Real healing. Deep healing. Spiritual healing. Healing that aligns with Scripture and brings you back to God's heart, not back into bondage.

The journey will require honesty, it will require courage, and the willingness to face truths you were taught to ignore. But every step you take will lead you closer to peace, freedom, and spiritual wholeness. This book is your invitation to breathe again. To lay down the guilt you've carried. To release the fear that has been gripping your heart. To reclaim the spiritual identity that was overshadowed by human error.

And as you read, ask yourself: what if God has been waiting for this exact moment to begin restoring the parts of you that you thought were gone forever? You are not here by accident. You are not reading these words by coincidence. Something in you is ready for truth. Something in you is ready for clarity. Something in you is ready for healing.

This book will not erase the past, but it will help you reclaim your future. A future where faith is not heavy. Where worship is not pressured. Where leadership is not oppressive. Where community is not toxic. Where God is not misrepresented. A future where you can breathe again. Where you can believe again. Where you can belong again.

Welcome to the beginning of a new chapter in your healing journey.

Chapter One:

Understanding Church Abuse

Defining Spiritual Abuse In The Body Of Christ

Spiritual abuse is real, and it is often wrapped in words like "submission", "authority", or "spiritual discipline". But before we chase labels or point fingers, let's give it a clear heart-level name you can hold. Spiritual abuse is the misuse of spiritual authority or biblical language to control, shame, silence, or exploit people, especially when those actions harm a person's relationship with God, themselves, or others. It hides behind piety and sometimes wears Sunday best. It can be loud or whisper-soft. Either way, it wounds.

Jesus Himself warned about leaders who burden people instead of helping them. He said of some religious leaders,

"They tie up heavy burdens and put them on people's shoulders, but they themselves are not willing to move them with one of their fingers"

(Matthew 23:4).

That image, heavy burdens strapped on you while the one who put them there walks by untouched, captures what spiritual abuse feels like. It is leadership that crushes instead of caring. Let's look at two scriptures close to the heart of this truth. Matthew 23:4 (above) describes leaders who impose burdens. Then listen to Peter, who calls leaders to shepherd willingly, "not lording it over those entrusted to you, but being examples to the flock" (1 Peter 5:2-3). The contrast is sharp: one approach burdens, the other tends. If leadership is meant to shepherd, spiritual abuse is the exact opposite; it is bleeding a flock rather than feeding it. Key terms to understand are:

- Authority (Greek: exousia): In Scripture, authority carries responsibility. The Greek word *'exousia'* points to power given for a purpose: to serve, to protect, and to guide. When that power is used to dominate, control, or silence, it becomes abusive.

- Submission is biblically given as an act of mutual love and order, not a ticket for someone to misuse you. Submission always sits under love; when love is missing, submission can turn into exploitation.

You need to know what spiritual abuse can look like in everyday life. Here are some common signs you might recognize:

- **Guilt-tripping that feels spiritual:** You are told God is angry with you unless you obey a leader's demand. Scripture may be quoted, but the heart is in control. Normal human behavior: people who want power will use language that sounds holy. For a change, ask whether the message leads you to God or to fear.

- **Information control and secrecy:** Decisions are made in closed rooms where accountability is thin. You are told not to question. Humans naturally protect status; churches should not. Insist on transparency; godly leadership flourishes in the light, not the dark.

- **Public shaming disguised as "correction":** Private matters are aired in a way that damages dignity. Healthy correction seeks restoration; shame destroys. You find social groups, police behavior, and gossip; churches must resist that temptation. The church should move toward restoration-focused correction, not humiliating exposure.

- **Fear as a motivator:** People obey because they are scared, for their reputation, standing, or perceived salvation. That's not faith; it is coercion. Humans respond to fear; spiritual maturity grows in trust. Replace fear tactics with teaching that grows conviction rather than compliance.

- **Spiritual bypassing of real pain:** "Pray more" becomes the response to abuse instead of offering listening, counselling, and accountability. Prayer is good, but it is not a substitute for justice or healing. Humans often prefer quick fixes; real care dwells with the hurt. Balance prayer with practical care, therapy, accountability, and restitution where needed.

- **Isolation and control of relationships:** You are discouraged from leaning on family or trusted friends; instead, you are told to stay within the leader's circle. Control thrives where isolation is created. Abusers separate people from help to tighten their grip. You need to keep your relational anchors, trusted family, godly friends, and counsellors close.

- **Charisma without character:** A leader may be gifted and powerful but lack humility. Gifts can seduce a congregation into ignoring harmful patterns. Remember: fruit matters.

People are drawn to charisma; your challenge is to test character and fruit, not charm.

Spiritual abuse grows where pride, fear, or insecurity go unexamined. It thrives in structures without checks and balances. Leaders who have a drive for recognition, control, or comfort can easily trade shepherding for ruling. When a culture confuses loyalty for a person with faithfulness to God, the soil becomes fertile for abuse. Add a community that fears conflict and values reputation above truth, and you get long seasons of hidden harm.

Biblical leaders were never meant to be unchecked. Paul wrote to the church, reminding elders to be examples and not tyrants (1 Peter 5:2-3). When we drift from that pattern, when leadership is about image, power, or wealth, hurt follows.

Spiritual abuse does not only cause hurt in the moment; it leaves marks. You may find yourself:

- Distrustful of leaders and fearful of community.

- Confused about God's character, was God harsh like that leader, or was that person misrepresenting him?

- Ashamed to share your story for fear of being judged or disbelieved.

- Quiet in prayer, or anxious in worship settings.

These are normal human reactions when trust is broken. The change needed is not just moving churches but tracking where your trust went wrong and rebuilding a healthy relationship with God and others.

If any of the signs above ring true, healing begins with naming what happened, not blaming yourself. You can say, "That was spiritual abuse." Speaking truth breaks the false power abuse has over you. Then, bring your hurt to safe people who listen without quick answers. Scripture, counselling, and community that honors boundaries are part of recovery.

Practical steps include: seeking a trusted counsellor, establishing safe boundaries, documenting incidents if needed, and finding a spiritual community that models servant leadership. Remember Jesus' model: leaders are shepherds, not overlords. The church is called to be a place of protection, not a place of added injury.

You are not obligated to tolerate spiritual harm. Recognizing abuse does not make you unspiritual; it makes you wise. You can love the church and still reject the ways it hurt you. You can hold Scripture close and still refuse to let anyone weaponize it against you. If you are reading this and you feel a mix of fear and relief, it is a good sign. That mix often marks the first step toward healing. You are naming what you felt but were told to ignore. You are beginning to separate God from the misrepresentation of people. In essence, you are opening the door to repair.

How Misuse of Authority Distorts The Image Of God

There is a quiet kind of damage that happens when someone in spiritual authority misrepresents God. It does not scream or leave visible wounds but it alters something deep inside you. It changes how you see God, how you hear God, and sometimes, how you trust God. When a leader, someone you respected, honored, or even feared, handled authority in a way God never intended, something in you began to shift. And often, you did not even know it was happening.

Many believers describe this as "losing sight of God", but what really happened was that the image of God was covered by the shadow of a human personality. Scripture shows us clearly that God reveals Himself as Shepherd, Father, Comforter, and Healer. But when someone who claims to represent Him behaves in ways that contradict His nature, your heart becomes confused. You start to wonder which version of God is real. This is why understanding the misuse of authority is so important. You cannot heal from something you cannot name. You cannot rebuild your picture of God until you see where it was distorted. The Bible tells us plainly in Jeremiah 23:1 (KJV),

"Woe be unto the pastors that destroy and scatter the sheep of my pasture, saith the Lord."

God does not ignore abusive leadership. He does not excuse their behavior. He confronts it. And He wants to free you from the effects of it.

Abusive leadership alters your understanding of God's character. When a leader acts in harsh, unpredictable, manipulative, or controlling ways, your heart slowly attaches those qualities to God. It is not something you decide to do, it happens quietly. If a pastor uses fear to control people, you may begin to think God is always angry or hard to please. If they shame you into obedience, you may start to believe that God only accepts you when you are perfect. If a leader punishes mistakes instead of correcting with love, you may assume God punishes before He listens.

It is human nature to interpret God through the lens of the people who lead us. From childhood, we learn about authority from the adults around us. If they were kind and patient, we tend to feel safe around authority. If they were unpredictable, we expect tension. So when a spiritual leader behaves in unhealthy ways, you subconsciously map their behavior onto God. This is why David cried in Psalm 27:10 (KJV), *"When my father and my mother forsake me, then the Lord will take me up."* David understood that human beings can fail painfully, but God's character remains different. God steps in to reveal Himself again, even when the ones who should have represented Him well failed.

Human control often hides the true nature of God's love and gentleness. The Hebrew word for love used often in scripture is "hesed", a word that means loyal love, covenant love, and love that refuses to let go. God's love is patient, steady, and deeply kind. But an abusive leader shifts your attention from that love to their own demands. It becomes easy to feel like God's heart is far away when, in truth, it is human behavior that blocked your sight.

A controlling leader will often say, "God told me to tell you," even when the instruction benefits them more than you. They may claim divine authority to make you feel guilty or afraid of questioning them. The problem is not that God speaks; He does. The danger is when leaders present their personal desire as God's voice. Over time, you begin to feel as though God is unapproachable. You start to believe that God only communicates through "special people" and that you are too small or too insignificant for Him to speak to directly.

But Jesus said in John 10:27 (KJV), *"My sheep hear my voice, and I know them, and they follow me."* Not "my pastors only", not "my prophets only". My sheep; ordinary believers, people like you. A controlling environment hides this truth. It makes you forget that God loves you and speaks to you personally. The truth is that when you experience repeated control, your mind learns to stay silent. You stop trusting yourself, you stop trusting what you hear from God, and you start waiting for someone else to approve your spiritual life. This is not freedom, it is spiritual dependency and it is the opposite of the relationship God desires with you.

One of the greatest dangers of abusive authority is equating God's voice with the voice of flawed leaders. When someone constantly says, "I am your covering," "God will punish you if you leave," or "You owe me loyalty," your heart becomes conditioned to hear their voice even when they are not speaking. Their tone becomes God's tone in your mind. Their threats become God's threats. Their manipulative statements become spiritual convictions. This is how spiritual trauma forms. You begin to fear God for the wrong reasons. You begin to obey out of anxiety instead of love. You begin to associate correction with humiliation and discipline with emotional pain.

But scripture shows us something different. When God speaks, He may challenge you, correct you, or convict you, but His voice always carries life. Even His correction brings hope. Hebrews 12:6 (KJV) says, *"For whom the Lord loveth he chasteneth."* God disciplines but never destroys. He corrects but never crushes.

A flawed leader may use your mistakes to establish control. God uses correction to strengthen your walk with Him. A leader may humiliate you, but God restores you. A leader may make you feel abandoned, but God draws you closer. This is why Jesus had to confront the Pharisees so strongly. They twisted God's laws into burdens. They added rules, they used fear and made people feel unworthy. Jesus came to reveal the true image of the Father: gentle, welcoming, full of truth and grace. When Jesus said in Matthew 11:28 (KJV),

"Come unto me, all ye that labor and are heavy laden, and I will give you rest,"

He was speaking to people who were spiritually exhausted by religious control. What He offered was the opposite of manipulation. He offered rest. When you realize that a human voice has overshadowed God's voice in your life, something beautiful begins to happen: your heart slowly turns back to the true Shepherd. You begin to see the difference between divine authority and human domination. You begin to recognize what is from God and what is simply personality, insecurity, fear, or manipulation. You begin to breathe again.

Healing starts when you allow God to separate Himself from the behaviors of flawed leaders. It starts when you hear His voice without the filter of fear. It starts when you rediscover that He is gentle, He is kind, He is patient, and He is not like the ones who wounded you. When you understand this, the journey to rebuilding your faith becomes possible again.

Chapter Two:

The Many Faces of Abuse In Church Settings

Pulpit Abuse: When Leadership Becomes Oppression

There is a reason God calls His servants shepherds. A shepherd guides, protects, leads, and feeds. A shepherd watches over the weak, tends to the wounded, carries the broken on his shoulder, and stands guard when wolves draw near. But something painful happens when a shepherd no longer reflects the heart of God. His voice becomes heavy instead of healing. His words become weapons instead of a stream. His presence starts to drain instead of strengthen. You begin to feel like you are walking on holy ground with bare feet and broken glass scattered everywhere. You love God, you respect spiritual authority, and you genuinely want to grow, but the atmosphere around the pulpit feels more like a courtroom than a sanctuary.

Pulpit abuse is one of the most damaging forms of spiritual harm because it disguises itself with holy language. It does not always shout; sometimes it whispers. It does not always threaten; sometimes it "corrects". It does not always command; sometimes it "advises". But one thing is always true: you walk away feeling smaller, not stronger. God becomes harder to recognize. Your own voice begins to fade and your spiritual life becomes something you survive instead of something you enjoy. Scripture speaks about this. Jesus warns us in Matthew 7:15:

"Beware of false prophets, which come to you in sheep's clothing, but inwardly they are ravenous wolves."

Notice the imagery: wolves dressed like sheep. They preach, they lead, they prophesy, but the fruit of their ministry burns instead of blessing. Another scripture, Ezekiel 34:4, says,

"The diseased have ye not strengthened, neither have ye healed that which was sick… but with force and with cruelty have ye ruled them."

Force and cruelty are two words God never associates with His nature. Let's walk through the layers of this type of abuse so you can finally put a name to what you've lived through.

When you sit under a pulpit that uses shame, fear, or embarrassment to "correct" you, your soul becomes tense. The sermon becomes a weapon. You start wondering, "Is he talking about me? Why does this feel like a public punishment?" A sermon should not feel like a spotlight shining on your flaws. It should feel like God's hand guiding you into truth with grace. But abusive sermons sound like warning shots fired at anyone who dares to think differently, question a decision, or step out of line.

You know, it is pulpit abuse when the message is less about Christ and more about control. Instead of feeding your spirit, the leader feeds his ego. Instead of lifting Jesus, he lifts himself, using the pulpit as a platform to silence, intimidate, or monitor people. The Word of God becomes a sword pointed at the congregation rather than a tool of healing. You sit there, stiff, trying not to breathe too loudly because you do not want to be the next example.

Have you ever noticed how some people leave church more afraid of their pastor than they are of the devil? That is what happens when charisma replaces character. Charisma is attractive; it moves people. But character transforms people. Charisma entertains; character shepherds. Charisma fills seats; character builds souls. Charisma without character is like a fire without a fireplace: beautiful to look at, but it burns everything it touches.

God never designed the pulpit to be a throne. A throne demands loyalty but a pulpit demands humility. When leadership shifts from servant-hearted to self-exalting, the whole spiritual environment changes. You begin to feel monitored instead of mentored. You feel evaluated instead of embraced. You learn to hide your weaknesses because weakness becomes a liability under a controlling leader. You measure your words, your expression, and even your worship because you do not want to be misunderstood or misjudged.

One dangerous sign of pulpit abuse is when a leader uses "prophecy" as a tool of manipulation. Suddenly, God always has something to say about your attitude, your giving, your loyalty, or your relationships, but never about their own behavior. The prophetic becomes a private CCTV camera. If you do not obey, you are "rebellious". If you do not agree, you are "Jezebel". If you do not comply, you are "not submissive". Yet 1 Corinthians 14:3 tells us that true prophecy *"edifies, exhorts, and comforts."* It does not control you; it guides you. It does not shrink your faith; it strengthens it. It does not make you fear leadership; it makes you love God more.

Another layer of pulpit abuse is correction that humiliates. Correction is biblical, public disgrace is not. Jesus corrected His disciples, but He never shamed them. He confronted sin, but He always restored dignity. But an oppressive leader uses correction as a microphone to broadcast your errors. Sometimes they won't mention your name, but the entire church knows who the sermon is aimed at. You feel the heat rise in your chest. You want to disappear under the chair. You begin to carry an emotional weight God never designed for you.

One Hebrew word relevant here is "ra'ah", which means "to feed, to shepherd". It is used in Psalm 23:1, "The Lord is my Shepherd." The idea is nourishment, guidance, and care. But abusive leaders turn shepherding into surveillance. They feed themselves, not the flock. They want your presence, your submission, your admiration, but not your growth. Because the more you grow, the harder it becomes to control you.

Fear becomes a tool. You start hearing threats wrapped in "love". You hear statements like, "Without me, you will fail." Or, "If you leave this covering, the enemy will attack you." When a leader positions himself as your only access to divine protection, you are dealing with spiritual manipulation. Leaders are meant to point you to God, not replace Him.

You'll also notice that under such leadership, joy dries up. You worship more from duty than desire. You serve more out of pressure than passion. You give more out of fear than faith. You stop hearing God clearly because every sermon sounds like the same warning: "Do not offend me." The pulpit becomes a prison and you start living like a prisoner who does not know how to escape.

But here is the truth God wants you to hold tightly: abusive leadership does not represent Him. God is not harsh. God is not controlling. God is not insecure. God is not manipulative. The Lord is gentle, patient, kind, slow to anger, abounding in mercy, and rich in compassion. Jesus said, *"My sheep hear my voice"* (John 10:27), not "My sheep are bullied into silence." You are not meant to serve God with fear lodged in your throat. You are meant to walk with Him boldly, freely, joyfully.

And if you have ever felt crushed, belittled, embarrassed, or spiritually suffocated under the sound of a pulpit that carried no love, you are not imagining it. Something was wrong. You were not oversensitive. You were not rebellious. You were not difficult. You were discerning something your spirit could not deny: the difference between the heart of a shepherd and the grip of a controller.

Congregational Abuse: When the Brethren Turn Into Accusers

There is a special kind of pain that comes from the pews. It sneaks up on you quietly because you never expect it. You expect love. You expect support. You expect fellowship. You expect the warmth of a spiritual family. But sometimes, instead of open arms, you meet folded arms. Instead of grace, you meet suspicion. Instead of encouragement, you meet whispers that travel faster than the Holy Spirit. And the place meant to be your refuge becomes the place you tiptoe around, careful not to breathe wrongly or be misunderstood.

Congregational abuse is one of the most underestimated forms of spiritual harm. People talk about abusive leaders and controlling pastors. But who talks about church members behaving like untrained ushers of judgment? Who talks about the cold looks, the side talks, and the cliques that form like private governments inside the church? Who talks about the whispers that wrap themselves around your confidence until you begin to shrink?

When the brethren, your supposed brothers and sisters in Christ, turn into accusers, something in your soul gets bruised in a place that is hard to explain. It is like being pricked by thorns inside a garden you thought was safe. You go there for life, but you encounter small deaths of the heart. Scripture does not ignore this. Psalm 55:12–14 says,

"For it was not an enemy that reproached me… But it was thou, a man mine equal, my guide, and mine acquaintance. We took sweet counsel together and walked unto the house of God in company."

That is the cry of a wounded believer. The pain is not from outsiders; it is from fellow worshippers. Another scripture, Galatians 5:15, warns, *"But if ye bite and devour one another, take heed that ye be not consumed one of another."* Bite. Devour. These are violent words, yet the apostle Paul used them for church members.

Let's take a walk through these layers of congregational abuse so you can recognize what your heart has been carrying.

Gossip is the first enemy, it is like smoke; it suffocates slowly, It spreads fast. And even after the fire is gone, the smell lingers. Gossip is not just talking; it is killing reputation by soft whispers. You notice it in the way conversations stop when you walk in. You notice it in the raised eyebrows. You notice it in the "prayer points" that sound suspiciously like people's personal issues packaged as intercession. Suddenly, everybody is praying about something you never told them.

Gossip creates an atmosphere where motives are questioned, mistakes are magnified, and people become topics instead of souls. It makes church feel like a marketplace of stories rather than a sanctuary of healing. Gossip is destructive because it is powered by imagination, not truth. It feeds on assumptions. It multiplies without evidence. And once it takes root, it spreads through the congregation like yeast in dough.

Then there are cliques, small circles within the larger circle. These are the unofficial tribes inside the church. They sit together, talk together, serve together, and subtly decide who belongs and who does not. Cliques create invisible fences. You see the friendliness, but you feel the closed door. They may not say, "You are not welcome," but their behavior says it. You find yourself standing alone during fellowship time, looking around for a place to fit in, but every corner is already taken. And nothing stings quite like feeling alone in a crowd of believers.

Cliques are dangerous because they create spiritual inequality. They give some people more voice, more influence, and more access, not because of righteousness but because of relationships. They turn church into a social club instead of a community of grace. And those who do not fit the image or the vibe end up on the margins, often ignored, overlooked, or silently judged.

Judgment is another heavy blow. Judgment is powerful because it wears the mask of righteousness. People will judge your clothing, your past, your mistakes, your vulnerability, your progress, your silence, and even your joy. They suddenly become self-appointed assessors of your spiritual life. Instead of seeing you as a human being growing at your own pace, they see you as a project that needs fixing or, worse, as a threat to their image of holiness.

Judgment strips away compassion. It removes the gentle heart needed to walk with people through pain. It creates a culture where everyone hides their struggles because showing weakness becomes dangerous. And when people judge you without knowing your story, you begin to guard your heart too tightly. You stop sharing. You stop trusting. You smile with your mouth but not with your eyes. You participate, but you do not connect. You live in the crowd but feel like a stranger in your own spiritual home.

How do church members become instruments of intimidation or exclusion? Very easily. Human nature has its flaws, and when spiritual maturity is missing, those flaws bloom wildly. People form opinions based on incomplete information. They follow the loudest voices. They seek belonging, even if it means aligning with harmful behavior. And because many do not understand their own authority in Christ, they adopt the behavior of whoever appears "spiritual" in the room.

Intimidation can look like sarcasm disguised as concern. It can look like subtle comments that remind you of your past. It can look like ignoring your contributions. It can look like giving you "that look" when you stand up to testify. It can look like members whispering about your decisions as if God did not give you your own mind. It can even look like church people acting like your personal Holy Spirit, monitoring your walk instead of cheering on your growth.

Exclusion, on the other hand, is quiet but painful. It is the empty chair beside you during programs. It is seeing others invited to hangouts you never hear about. It is realizing that when it comes to weddings, naming ceremonies, fellowships, or even prayer groups, your name never appears on the list. It is hearing about plans long after they have already happened. And the message becomes clear: "You do not fit."

Being wounded by spiritual family is one of the hardest things to heal from because it touches something deep: your trust in the idea of community. You wonder why the same people who shout "love your neighbor" on Sunday can treat you like an inconvenience by Monday. You wonder why people who teach forgiveness struggle to practice it. You wonder why the church that preached acceptance made you feel like a burden. Maybe you've carried that confusion quietly. Maybe you even blamed yourself. But hear this clearly: you were not wrong to expect love. You were not wrong to desire belonging. You were not wrong to hope for acceptance. God created the church to be a family, not a battlefield.

The Greek word for "brethren" is *adelphoi,* meaning "from the same womb". That's powerful. It means we are meant to share spiritual DNA, not spiritual daggers. When brethren become accusers, they stop acting like the church Jesus designed. But here is the good news: God sees every tear caused by careless words. God notices every wound caused by judgmental glances. God hears every sigh you've released in the parking lot before walking into the sanctuary, and He is not neutral. He is your healer, your defender, your comforter.

You are not invisible or overreacting, you are not difficult, are you imagining the pain. You were wounded in a place that was supposed to heal you. But you will not stay wounded. God is restoring your confidence, cleaning the wounds others caused and calling you back to a love that is real, pure, and gentle. You will find your people. You will find your tribe. You will find your true spiritual family.

Chapter Three:

The Silent Exodus: Why Believers Leave Church

Walking Away To Preserve Spiritual Sanity

There comes a moment when your soul begins to whisper the truth you've been afraid to say out loud. A moment when the noise around you becomes so loud that your spirit starts drowning under the weight of "church expectations". You sit in a service and feel your chest tighten, not because the Holy Spirit is convicting you, but because something inside you is suffocating. You hear familiar words – grace, holiness, obedience – but they no longer sound like life. They sound like chains. And you wonder, quietly, secretly, "Lord, is something wrong with me?" Nothing is wrong with you. Sometimes leaving is not rebellion; it is survival. The Bible says in Psalm 34:18,

"The Lord is near to the brokenhearted and saves those who are crushed in spirit."

Notice that God draws close when your spirit is crushed. He does not accuse you or shame you, He rescues you. And sometimes His rescue looks like you stepping away from what is breaking you. When staying in a place keeps crushing your spirit instead of strengthening it, God is not the one holding you there.

Walking away from a harmful church environment is not about abandoning God. It is about refusing to abandon your soul. You were never designed to stay where your spiritual sanity is bleeding out. God did not call you to endurance without wisdom. He did not call you to loyalty without discernment. He did not call you to a spiritual community that drains the very life Jesus came to give you.

You remember His words in John 10:10, "I came that they may have life, and have it abundantly." If what you are experiencing feels like spiritual starvation instead of abundant life, then something is wrong with the environment, not your desire for peace. Some believers leave because the atmosphere becomes toxic to their spiritual lungs. They keep inhaling manipulation, guilt, and pressure, and after a while, their soul starts wheezing. That is not spiritual immaturity; that is human reality. You cannot breathe in poison and expect your spirit to remain healthy. You cannot sit under manipulation and still flourish. You cannot feed on fear and grow in love. It is simply impossible.

Imagine a plant placed in a room with no sunlight. No matter how much you water it, speak to it, or hope for the best, it will still bend, weaken, and eventually collapse. The problem is not the plant; it is the environment. In the same way, you may have been trying to grow in a place with no genuine light. A place where the "sun" is blocked by human ego, harsh control, unhealthy expectations, and spiritual theatrics that have nothing to do with Christ.

When you leave such a place, you are not running from God, you are running toward light. Many believers carry heavy guilt when they consider stepping away. It is the kind of guilt that clings to your conscience like smoke after a fire. You hear old sermons in your mind telling you that leaving means you are disloyal, rebellious, ungrateful, or spiritually weak. You hear voices, maybe even from people you trusted, saying that "a real believer stays no matter what."

But staying in a place that destroys you is not loyalty, it is self-neglect. God never asked you to sacrifice your mental health on the altar of someone else's definition of commitment. He never asked you to stay silent under pressure just to "honor leadership". He never asked you to diminish your voice to keep everyone comfortable. He never asked you to obey a system at the expense of your soul.

What God does ask is simple: "Guard your heart" (Proverbs 4:23). The Hebrew word for "guard" here is *natsar*, which means to keep, preserve, and protect from danger. When you walk away from a spiritually harmful environment, you are guarding your heart in obedience to God's command. You are not disobeying Scripture, you are obeying it.

And yet the guilt remains heavy for many. Why? Because you were told, implicitly or directly, that the church is the one place you must never walk away from. That if you leave, somehow your salvation is at risk or your spiritual life will crumble. But the church is not a physical building. The church is not an organization with a registration number. The church is not a personality on a stage. The church is not a particular style of worship or a particular set of rituals. The church is the body of Christ. And Christ goes where you go.

When you leave a harmful environment, God does not stay behind on the altar. He walks out with you. Sometimes you discover that the environment you left was slowly draining you. You begin to see yourself again, your joy, your voice, your peace. You start to sleep better. You pray without fear again. You breathe without tension. You read Scripture without hearing someone's voice in your head twisting it to control you. Your spiritual lungs open, and you realize how much you were suffocating.

Leaving becomes your first step toward healing. It becomes your first act of spiritual self-respect. It becomes your first move toward freedom. You also begin to realize that your decision was not a moment of weakness but a moment of awakening. That God was nudging you all along. That your discomfort was not rebellion but revelation. That the Holy Spirit was showing you: "You cannot heal where you are being wounded."

Here is the truth most people won't admit: many believers who leave toxic church environments love God deeply. Their problem was never with Jesus. Their wound came from His representatives. And because the pain came from people wearing His name, it felt almost impossible to separate the love of God from the behavior of men.

But once you step away, your vision clears. You begin to see God again, without filters. You begin to feel His tenderness. You rediscover His voice, the gentle one, not the harsh one. You realize He never spoke to you with intimidation, neither did He place chains on your conscience. His voice was always kind, always healing, and always life-giving. Isaiah 42:3 says,

"*A bruised reed He will not break, and a smoldering wick He will not quench.*"

If God refuses to break what is already bruised, why would He ask you to stay where others keep breaking you? Sometimes you walk away not because you lost faith, but because you refused to lose your mind.

And here is the prophetic truth: God will meet you outside the walls, He always has. He met Moses outside Egypt. He met Elijah outside the noise of Israel. He met Hagar in the wilderness. He met the Samaritan woman outside the religious centers of her day. God has never been allergic to your exit. So if you left for survival, breathe again. Heaven is not angry with you. You are not a prodigal. You are not a failure. You are not faithless. You are simply someone who refused to die internally while pretending to be fine externally. Walking away was your first step toward life again.

The Emotional, Mental, And Spiritual Weight Of Staying Silent

Silence is heavy. You feel it even before you can explain it. It sits on your chest, presses on your voice, and squeezes your courage until you convince yourself that saying nothing is safer than saying the truth. When you are inside a toxic church environment, silence becomes a survival strategy. You tell yourself, "If I just keep quiet, maybe the storm will pass." But storms do not disappear because you whisper. They only grow bigger, darker, and closer.

You've probably been there, watching things you knew were wrong, yet swallowing your words because speaking up felt like carrying fire in your hands. Maybe you did not want to offend anyone. Maybe you were afraid of the backlash. Maybe you did not want to be labelled rebellious, carnal, or ungrateful. Maybe you wanted peace, not trouble. So you stayed quiet and hoped it would get better. But silence has a price. Scripture shows us that hidden pain becomes a trap. David said,

"When I kept silent, my bones wasted away through my groaning all day long"

(Psalm 32:3).

Silence did not heal him. Silence drained him. Silence broke him from the inside. That's what happens to you when you are hurting in church but feel too afraid to say it. You convince yourself you are protecting unity, but in reality, you are sacrificing your emotional and spiritual health on the altar of appearances.

One of the biggest reasons people stay silent is fear: fear of punishment, fear of rejection, fear of being misunderstood, fear of being gossiped about, and fear of losing their place in a community that once felt like home. Fear builds an invisible cage around your voice. You know the words are there. You know the truth burns inside you. But fear whispers, "If you speak, they will turn against you." That whisper becomes a leash around your heart.

The truth is, many believers who experience abuse do not speak out because they've seen what happens to those who try. They've seen church members become hostile. They've seen people humiliated publicly, isolated privately, or spiritually threatened: "Touch not the Lord's anointed." They've seen leaders preach entire sermons that target a single individual while pretending it is "the Spirit leading." When you witness this kind of retaliation, silence feels like the only safe option. But is it truly safe?

Silence does not protect you. It protects the system that hurts you. And that realization is painful. Because in your heart, you want peace, not war. You want Jesus, not chaos. Yet the more you hold your pain inside, the more that pain begins to shape your emotions. You begin to feel anxious in church. Your mind becomes crowded with thoughts you cannot process. Your body reacts. Your worship becomes mechanical. Your prayers feel shallow. Your joy dries up. Like David, your "bones waste away".

Silence builds walls. It isolates you even when you are surrounded by people. You can be in church every week yet feel completely alone because no one knows what you carry. The human heart is not designed to hold secrets this heavy. The human mind is not built to carry pain in solitary confinement. That's why the Bible commands us to "confess your faults one to another, and pray one for another, that you may be healed" (James 5:16). Healing requires expression. Healing requires honesty. Healing requires a voice.

But for many believers, silence becomes a spiritual conflict. You feel torn between loyalty to the church and loyalty to yourself. One part of you says, "Do not say anything. It will cause trouble." Another part of you whispers, "If you stay silent, you will break." And in that confusion, you begin to wonder if speaking up makes you a bad Christian. But the truth is this: protecting your mental and spiritual well-being is not rebellion. It is wisdom. Jesus Himself withdrew from places and people who refused truth or brought unnecessary danger. Why should you be less wise?

You see, silence also feeds shame. When you do not talk about what happened to you, you start blaming yourself for it. You assume you are overreacting. You assume your discernment was wrong. You assume you are weak for feeling wounded. Shame blankets your identity until you start believing you deserved what you went through. That's the danger of silent suffering: the enemy loves quiet places because he can plant lies there.

And spiritually, silence creates a fog. You lose clarity. You lose confidence. You lose the courage to trust your own discernment. You begin to equate suffering with faithfulness. You think God expects you to tolerate pain without complaint. But nowhere in Scripture does God ask you to be silent under oppression. Jesus confronted injustice. Paul confronted Peter. Nathan confronted David. Silence was never the path to healing in God's kingdom.

There is also the mental pressure. You carry the weight of unspoken words. You replay experiences in your mind. You analyze conversations. You doubt your instincts. Your nervous system becomes overactive because you are constantly trying to predict the next harmful moment. And because you cannot express your truth, your body stores it. Trauma becomes a physical memory. It shows up in your breathing, your sleep, your appetite, your mood, and your focus. Silence does not just affect your spirit. It affects your whole self.

For some believers, silence becomes a spiritual drought. You want to pray but do not know how. You open your Bible, but the words feel distant. You worship, but your heart feels numb. You begin to think God is far away, but in reality, the silence has suffocated your ability to breathe spiritually. God is near, but your pain has not been spoken, so it has not been released. God cannot heal what you constantly hide.

At some point, there is a moment of awakening, a prophetic jolt in your spirit. You realize something is wrong; staying silent is slowly killing your peace. You realize silence is not strength.

Silence is bondage. And you know deep inside that God never meant for you to survive His house; He meant for you to flourish in it. So here is the truth you must hold tight: your voice matters. Your story matters. God never asked you to protect the image of a flawed system. He asked you to guard your heart. He asked you to walk in truth. He asked you to pursue peace, not pretend peace. And if speaking out is the step that leads you toward freedom, then heaven stands with you.

This is your wake-up moment. No more silent suffering. No more invisible wounds. No more sitting in the shadows while your soul bleeds. The God who sees you also hears you. He is not threatened by your truth. He is not offended by your pain. He is not disappointed in your need for healing. You are not breaking the church by speaking out, but you are breaking the chains that tried to silence you, and that is holy.

Chapter Four:

When Honour is Manipulated

The Difference between Biblical Submission and Blind Loyalty

There is a kind of honor that brings life, and there is a kind that quietly steals the breath out of your soul. One comes from God. The other comes from fear, pressure, and manipulation dressed in religious language. And if you have ever questioned whether you were honoring a leader "correctly" or wondered if God was displeased because you could not obey a human being blindly, then this chapter will meet you exactly where you are.

The truth is simple: **God never designed spiritual submission to be slavery.** The God who formed Adam from the dust did not breathe His life into you only for you to shrink into a corner because someone behind a pulpit said, "Touch not my anointed." Submission in Scripture looks nothing like the heavy obedience demanded by insecure people. It looks like love. It looks like humility. It looks like Christ.

But let's start at the foundation, which is to understand what biblical submission really means. The Bible uses the word *'submit'* often, but the heart behind it is mutual honor, not forced allegiance. Ephesians 5:21 says, *"Submit yourselves one to another in the fear of God."* Notice the instruction, **one to another.** Leaders included. Pastors included. Apostles included. The flock included. Everyone standing before God in humility.

The Greek word for "submit" in this verse is *hupotassō*, a military term that means "to arrange under", but not in the sense of "be crushed under". It means to willingly take your place in order, out of respect and cooperation. It is about harmony, not hierarchy. It is about unity, not domination. It is about carrying the weight together, not placing it all on the shoulders of the weaker one.

When God calls you to submit, He is not telling you to surrender your will, your mind, or your ability to hear Him. He is asking you to walk in love and humility, the same way Christ did. Jesus submitted to the Father out of love, not fear. And that is how biblical submission works; **it flows from relationship, not intimidation.**

Real submission feels safe. It feels light. It feels like standing under a covering that protects you, not a burden that crushes you. It allows you to be honest. It allows you to grow. It allows you to say "yes" with joy and "no" with clarity.

But blind loyalty? That's a different story entirely.

Manipulative leaders know exactly how to twist the word "honor". They wrap it like a rope around the necks of sincere believers who only want to please God. A simple verse becomes a weapon. A sermon becomes a chain. A prophecy becomes a leash. And suddenly, what God designed to be beautiful becomes a tool of domination.

Blind loyalty says, "Do whatever I say." "Never question me." "If you disagree, you are rebellious." "If you leave, you are cursed." "Your blessing is tied to my voice." None of these ideas reflect the nature of Jesus. Not one. Jesus never said, "Follow me, and do not ask questions." He invited people into truth. He corrected with clarity, not confusion. He washed the feet of His followers, not the other way around. When a leader becomes untouchable, unquestionable, uncorrectable, and unreachable, something has gone very wrong.

Peter was corrected by Paul publicly (Galatians 2:11–14). Yet God still honored Peter's calling. Why? Because correction does not destroy an anointed person; **pride does**.

If your spiritual leader reacts to accountability like a vampire reacts to sunlight, you are dealing with control, not biblical leadership.

How Leaders Use Honor To Silence You

One of the easiest ways to control believers is to turn "honor" into a fear-based performance. You begin to feel that you must constantly prove your loyalty. You second-guess your intentions. You walk on eggshells, hoping your leader does not misinterpret your facial expression. And before you know it, "honor" becomes a never-ending list of sacrifices: Your time. Your money. Your sleep. Your boundaries. Your identity. Your voice.

You stop saying "I feel uncomfortable," because you are told it means you lack submission. You stop asking questions because you are told it means you are prideful. You stop thinking for yourself because you are told that "thinking too much" disrupts the move of God.

Bit by bit, honor is used to shrink you until you fit a mold that looks less like Christ and more like the preferences of a human being. But God did not call you to be a shadow of someone else. He called you to be a witness of Him. The truth that may shock many of us is that **you can honor a leader and still say no.** You can honor a church and still set boundaries. You can honor a pastor and still disagree respectfully. God does not expect you to amputate your identity to keep someone else comfortable.

Real honor protects dignity. It does not erase it. This is why Shadrach, Meshach, and Abednego could respect King Nebuchadnezzar but refuse to bow (Daniel 3). They were honorable. They were respectful. But they knew their final loyalty belonged to God, not a man, even a powerful one. The same principle applies today. Honoring God means walking in truth, even when truth is uncomfortable. Honoring God means guarding your heart, even when others call it rebellion. Honoring God means standing before Jesus with your conscience intact, not shattered by religious pressure.

A leader who insists you obey them above God is a leader who has lost the fear of God. A church that punishes questions is a church that has lost the voice of the Holy Spirit. A system that demands silence is a system that has abandoned truth. God does not need you to disappear in order for His glory to appear.

You Are Not Wrong for Wanting Safety. If you feel confused when someone preaches about honor, if you feel a knot in your stomach, if your heart races, if you feel pressured instead of inspired, it is not rebellion. It is discernment. It is your spirit recognizing that something is off. Submission should feel like being guided, not being choked. Honor should feel like love, not like a trap, and obedience should feel like wisdom, not like bondage.

And if you've ever wondered, "Is it me? Am I the problem? "Am I dishonoring God by resisting?" The answer is usually no. What you are resisting isn't God. It is manipulation packaged as spirituality. The One who saved you is not threatened by your humanity. He invites it. He welcomes it. He formed your mind. He shaped your conscience. And He never asks you to bow so low to a human that you no longer recognize yourself. Biblical submission is freedom. Blind loyalty is captivity. You were not called to be a slave in the house of your Father. You were called to be a son, a daughter, walking in truth, in courage, and in honor that reflects Christ, not fear.

How False Doctrines Create Psychological Bondage

You can sit in a church for years, hear the name of Jesus every Sunday, lift your hands during worship, and still feel like you are suffocating inside. Not because God is far, but because the doctrines being poured over your soul are quietly building a prison around your mind. False doctrines do not always look dangerous at first. They often come dressed in spiritual language, soaked in Scripture quotes, and wrapped in a tone of authority. They sound holy, but they do not smell like Christ. They sound deep, but they do not lead you to freedom. They sound spiritual, but they chain your emotions with fear, guilt, and confusion.

This is why Paul warned the church, "Let no one deceive you with empty words" (Ephesians 5:6). Empty words do not mean the preacher said nothing. It means the words **lacked the life of Christ**. They may have been loud, impressive, dramatic, or full of claims, but they did not carry the truth that sets free. Jesus said, *"You will know the truth, and the truth will make you free"* (John 8:32).

Meaning: anything that does the opposite is not His voice. False doctrines create psychological bondage because they shift your focus from Christ to men, from grace to fear, from relationship to performance, and from discernment to dependence. Let's break this down.

You were never created to live under the weight of human perfection. You were never asked to carry the pressure of pleasing a spiritual leader at the expense of your peace. You were never designed to obey out of terror. Fear may control behavior for a while, but it does not transform the heart. Only love does that. Yet, many churches today preach fear as if God outsourced His personality to intimidation.

Some doctrines elevate leaders so highly that questioning them feels like questioning God Himself. You may have heard statements like, "If you leave this church, your life will scatter." "If you disagree with me, you are resisting God." "If you do not submit completely, you are breaking spiritual covering." "If you do not sow into my life, you are robbing yourself of blessing."

These are not teachings of Christ, they are tools of manipulation. They create psychological bondage because they silence your ability to think, discern, or disagree. They create a mental cage where you second-guess your own spiritual instincts. You forget how to hear God for yourself. You begin to believe that your safety depends on a human being. You lose your sense of self. Slowly, your inner world becomes ruled not by the Holy Spirit, but by the fear of punishment, rejection, or curses.

But Jesus never taught His disciples to fear Him in that way. The fear of the Lord (Hebrew: *yirah*, deep reverence, awe) is not terror.

It is honor rooted in love. Notice the difference. Terror shuts the heart. Reverence opens it. False doctrines twist this and replace reverence with dread.

Let's talk about teachings that elevate leaders above accountability. Some pastors stand in God's house but behave as if they own it. They preach as though they are the exclusive channel of divine revelation. They position themselves so high that nobody can ask questions, raise concerns, or hold them accountable. When leaders place themselves above correction, people under them slowly feel smaller, weaker, and unworthy. You begin to feel like you must win their approval to keep your spiritual standing. You start to see them as spiritual giants and yourself as spiritually incompetent. This is psychological bondage.

But the Bible never places any man above correction. Not even Paul. Not even Peter. Peter was publicly corrected by Paul (Galatians 2:11). Leaders are shepherds, not gods. Shepherds guide the sheep; they do not become the lord of the sheep. When a doctrine elevates a leader to the place where they cannot be questioned, that doctrine is not biblical. It is idolatry.

Fear-based teachings also imprison the mind. When every sermon feels like a threat, your spiritual life becomes a battlefield of anxiety. You no longer read Scripture to know God; you read it to avoid punishment. You no longer serve from joy; you serve from fear of being labelled rebellious. You stop thinking for yourself. You silence your own discernment. You shrink. You hide. You comply, but you are not growing, you are surviving. This is why the Scripture says,

> ***"God has not given us a spirit of fear, but of power, love, and a sound mind" (2 Timothy 1:7).***

A sound mind means a mind that can think clearly, discern wisely, and choose freely. If a doctrine strips these away, it is not from God.

Fear-based doctrines sound like this: "If you miss one service, the devil will attack you." "If you do not sow every week, your finances will dry up." "If you question the 'man of God', your life will be cursed." "If you do not obey your spiritual father, God won't bless you."

Let me tell you plainly: **these are lies**. They are spiritual intimidation dressed as truth. Christ did not die to make you a slave again. He died to make you free.

Fear-based doctrines also attack your emotions. They make you feel unworthy, guilty, and constantly anxious. You begin to feel spiritually insecure. You start believing that God is always disappointed with you. This creates emotional exhaustion. Over time, emotional exhaustion becomes spiritual burnout. You begin to dread church instead of looking forward to it. You go, but your soul stays home. You serve, but your peace resigns. Eventually, you feel trapped in a cycle of fear, guilt, and silence. This is psychological bondage. But how do you break free?

First, you must return to the heart of Christ. Study the words of Jesus Himself. He never manipulated, or threatened, He was never controlled instead He invited. He called and drew people with love. Every doctrine must be measured against the character of Christ. If it oppresses, it is not Him. If it shames, it is not Him. If it crushes, it is not Him. If it silences your voice, it is not Him. If it elevates a leader above accountability, it is not Him.

Second, surround yourself with truth. The Word of God is a hammer that breaks chains but also a light that exposes lies. When you feed your mind truth, lies lose their grip. When you rebuild your relationship with the Holy Spirit, you slowly regain confidence in hearing God for yourself. You begin to trust your spiritual instincts again.

Third, allow yourself to heal. Breaking free from false doctrine is not just a mental shift, it is emotional recovery. It takes time to unlearn fear. It takes time to rediscover joy. It takes time to believe again that God loves you without conditions.

You are not weak for being affected. You were hurt because you trusted. And God will honor that trust by healing you. Just remember that any doctrine that contradicts the heart of Christ is a chain waiting to be broken, and you have God's permission to break it. You were made for freedom and freedom is coming back to you now in Jesus' name. Amen.

Chapter Five:

Trauma in the House of God

Recognizing Church-Induced Trauma

You may not realize it at first but trauma in a church setting does not always walk up to you wearing a name tag. It does not always come with bruises anyone can see. Sometimes it hides behind your worship songs, your "I'm fine", and your ability to keep showing up even when your heart is limping. Church-induced trauma is one of the most silent wounds a believer can carry. And because it happens in a place you were told should be safe, the confusion cuts even deeper. Pain feels heavier when it is unexpected.

When Jesus said in Matthew 11:28, *"Come unto Me, all ye that labor and are heavy laden, and I will give you rest,"* He wasn't just speaking to people burdened with sin. He was speaking to anyone carrying weight, including the weight of experiences that happened in His name but were never from His heart. Trauma is any wound that overwhelms your ability to cope. And when it happens in church, it burrows into the emotional, mental, and spiritual parts of your being all at once.

Church trauma has symptoms, and until you recognize them, you may blame yourself for "not being spiritual enough," when in reality, you are simply hurting. One of the clearest signs of church-induced trauma is emotional conflict. You feel a deep sadness when thinking about church. You feel anxious before services. Or you feel numb, like someone drained the color out of your faith life. But instead of identifying these emotions for what they are, responses to hurt, you may assume it is "spiritual dryness".

Many believers say things like, "I do not feel God anymore," when the real issue is that they were wounded by people who misrepresented Him. Trauma plays tricks on your emotions. It tells you that avoiding pain means avoiding God. It whispers guilt into your heart for stepping away from what hurt you.

Psalm 34:18 says, *"The Lord is near to the brokenhearted and saves the crushed in spirit."* Notice He did not say, "The Lord is near to the rebellious." He said the brokenhearted. If your heart feels crushed, it is not because God abandoned you. It may simply be that someone mishandled it.

Some believers stop serving, stop volunteering, or step back from ministries they once loved and immediately feel like they have failed God. But stepping back is not rebellion, sometimes it is recovery. This is because church trauma caused by church abuse often disguises itself as disinterest. You do not want to pray because the last time you prayed with a group, someone shamed you. You do not want to join a department because the last department drained your soul. You do not want to sit in the same space where manipulation happened. Your mind calls it "laziness", but your heart is simply avoiding danger.

When Elijah fled from Jezebel in 1 Kings 19, he wasn't rebellious. He was exhausted, frightened, and traumatized. Yet God did not scold him. God fed him, strengthened him, and spoke to him gently. That is what love does: it heals before it instructs. Trauma makes your spirit sit down long before your legs do.

There is also the symptom of hyper-vigilance in spiritual spaces. You walk into church, but your body is on alert. Your heart beats fast for no reason. You scan the room like someone waiting for the next explosion. You are not paranoid; you are wounded. Hyper-vigilance is a trauma response. When you have been spiritually or emotionally mishandled, your nervous system stays on guard. You may find yourself reacting strongly to harmless comments because they remind you of past hurts. A simple correction feels like punishment. A leader calling your name feels like a threat. You flinch when someone says, "Can I see you after service?" This is trauma speaking. It is the voice of memories your body has not forgotten.

When trauma happens under spiritual authority, the confusion doubles. You trusted someone. You believed they represented God. When they hurt you, manipulated you, or dismissed your pain, your heart did not know where to place the betrayal. So it placed it on itself. Church trauma often grows in the soil of misplaced guilt.

You think, "I should have spoken up." "I should have been stronger." "I should have forgiven quicker." "I shouldn't feel this way."

But guilt is not the language of the Holy Spirit. Conviction draws you to God. Guilt pushes you away from Him. Shame locks your voice. Trauma convinces you that protecting yourself is dishonor. You must remind yourself: Jesus never shamed the wounded.

When trauma is present, your emotions feel tired. You cry easily or not at all. Small tasks feel heavy. You may even develop symptoms like headaches, irritability, or difficulty sleeping. These are not signs of weak faith. They are signs of a weary soul. The

Hebrew word for soul, *nephesh,* means "the inner being", "the breath", or "the life within". Trauma does not just affect your mind; it affects your *nephesh.* It drains your inner life. And once the inner life is tired, everything, prayer, worship, even reading Scripture, feels like climbing a hill with a stone tied to your chest.

There is a feeling of being unsafe in the presence of God. This one is subtle but deep. When trauma happens in church, you may unconsciously connect God with the atmosphere where the pain happened. You know He wasn't the one who hurt you, but your emotions struggle to separate the two. You may hesitate to pray, you may feel nervous during worship, you may not know how to talk to God without thinking about what happened. Trauma distorts your spiritual compass. It makes the house of God feel like a battlefield. But remember this truth: God is not the pain you experienced. He is the healer entering the pain.

Church trauma makes you second-guess yourself. You question every decision, every thought, and every boundary. When you were ignored, controlled, or gaslit in spiritual spaces, your confidence absorbed the blow. This confusion is not weakness; it is a symptom. When spiritual leaders mishandle authority, people begin to believe they cannot hear God on their own. But Jesus said in John 10:27, *"My sheep hear My voice."* This includes you. Even wounded sheep hear their Shepherd.

You cannot heal what you cannot name. Recognizing trauma does not mean you are dishonoring the church. It means you are protecting the temple of God that you are. Your healing matters to God. Your emotions matter to God. Your story matters to God. Awareness is the first doorway to freedom, and you deserve freedom.

The Long-Term Effects of Being Wounded In A Place of Worship

There is a special kind of wound that forms when the place meant to heal you becomes the place that hurts you. A wound from a stranger stings, but a wound from a spiritual family goes deeper. A wound from an outsider can be brushed off, but a wound from a leader you trusted can feel like it tears something inside your soul. These long-term effects do not just disappear because you prayed once or because someone told you to "move on". Trauma in a place of worship affects you slowly, quietly, and in layers, like a shadow that follows you long after you have left the building.

The first thing you must understand is that spiritual wounds are real wounds. They affect every part of a person: mind, emotions, spirit, relationships, belief systems, and even identity. When David cried in Psalm 55:12–14 about betrayal from a close companion, he wasn't exaggerating. His heart recognized the truth we often try to hide: wounds from familiar places cut the deepest. And the impact does not fade quickly.

Let's walk through these long-term effects carefully so you can recognize what has been happening in you or someone you love.

A shaken sense of trust: Trust is the foundation of any healthy relationship, especially a relationship with God. When someone in spiritual authority breaks trust, your mind does not simply limit that betrayal to the individual. It spills over. Suddenly, you struggle to trust other leaders, other believers, and even well-meaning people who genuinely want to help. You begin to wonder, "What if this one is also pretending?" "What if I open up and they use my words against me?" "What if kindness is just a trap?" Trust becomes something you protect instead of something you give. This is because the brain interprets repeated hurt as danger. When a spiritual environment misuses authority, your nervous system remembers the fear and catalogues it under "church", "pastor", "prophecy", or "fellowship". You aren't being dramatic; you are responding to previous pain. It takes time to rebuild trust, and that's okay. God is patient with your rebuilding process.

A wounded prayer life: This is one of the most painful long-term effects, because it is not always obvious at first. When church trauma happens, your mind knows that God is different from the people who hurt you, but your emotions have not yet caught up. So prayer becomes something you struggle with, not because you do not love God, but because the place where the wound happened and the presence of God got mixed up in your heart.

For some believers, prayer becomes dry. For others, prayer becomes heavy. For many, prayer becomes a battlefield of memories. Your heart wants to draw near, but your emotions hesitate. You come to God carrying memories that should never have been part of your spiritual journey. You may even begin to feel unworthy, like your voice has no weight before Him. But here is the truth: your wounded voice is still a beloved voice. Psalm 147:3 says, *"He heals the brokenhearted and binds up their wounds."* He never abandons a bleeding heart. Not once.

A damaged sense of spiritual identity: One of the greatest attacks of church trauma is against your identity. Leaders who misuse authority often speak words that belittle, diminish, or confuse you. These words do not just float away. They sink. And sometimes they stay lodged in your heart for years.

Suddenly questions start rising:

"Am I really called?" "Maybe I'm not spiritual enough." "Maybe God is disappointed in me." "Maybe something is wrong with me."

Trauma makes you rewrite your identity through the lens of your pain instead of the truth of Scripture. But in Ephesians 2:10, God already called you *His workmanship.* The Greek word there is *poiēma,* meaning "a masterpiece", "a crafted work", or "a poem formed with intention". Trauma may distort your reflection, but it cannot rewrite God's original design.

Relationship difficulties: Church trauma does not stay inside the church, it follows you into friendships, marriage, family, and even your workplace. You may become overly cautious. You may struggle to let people close. You may constantly wait for betrayal. You may start building walls so high that no one, not even those who love you, can climb them. This is because spiritual wounds alter your perception of connection. You were hurt in a place that was meant to represent unconditional love. So part of your heart begins to question if unconditional love exists at all. Over time, you may notice that:

You avoid deep conversations. You fear being vulnerable. You cut people off quickly to avoid disappointment. You prefer emotional distance to emotional risk. These are not character flaws. These are survival patterns. But survival patterns must eventually give way to healing patterns.

Inner vows and silent promises: When someone is hurt deeply in a church setting, they often make silent vows: "I'll never trust a pastor again." "I'll never join a department again." "I'll never submit to leadership again." "I'll never open up again." These vows feel protective at first. They give you a sense of control. But over time, they become emotional prisons. They limit what God wants to do in your life. They block genuine relationships. They interfere with destiny connections. God does not want you living behind emotional walls. He wants you healed enough to choose wisely, not wounded enough to hide endlessly.

Long-term spiritual confusion: Another major long-term effect is confusion about who God really is. When abuse or manipulation is done "in the name of God", the image of God becomes distorted. You may start seeing Him as harsh, unpredictable, unstable, or impossible to please, because that is how abusive leaders behave. This confusion can lead to fear of making mistakes, fear of disappointing God, fear of judgment, and fear of spiritual authority. But God is not the author of confusion. And He is nothing like those who misrepresented Him. His voice brings life, clarity, and peace, not intimidation.

A deep desire for God mixed with fear of His people: This is one of the strangest and most painful contradictions. Trauma makes you love God deeply but fear the people who claim to represent Him. You want fellowship, but you fear being hurt again. You want community, but you fear exposure. You want accountability, but you fear control. This tension can last for years. But healing is possible. Slowly, gently, God begins to separate Himself from what you went through. He begins to reintroduce Himself, not as a harsh overseer but as a tender Father.

The need for intentional restoration: time does not heal church trauma. Silence does not heal it. Avoidance does not heal it. True healing requires intentional restoration spiritually, emotionally, and mentally. You may need to talk about what happened, to grieve the loss, to rebuild your spiritual confidence, to relearn the voice of God or to allow safe people to walk with you. You need to understand that healing is not a betrayal of your past loyalty. Healing is obedience to God's desire for your wholeness. And just as Psalm 23:3 says, *"He restores my soul."* Restoration is not a suggestion, it is part of your covenant.

Chapter Six:

When Shepherds Bleed the Sheep

Understanding Narcissistic, Controlling, and Insecure Leadership

There is something heartbreaking about watching someone who was called to heal become the one who wounds. You walk into church expecting a shepherd, but sometimes you find a wounded warrior wearing a crown he never healed enough to carry. And because leadership is a magnifier, whatever is unhealed in a leader often spills into those who follow. You begin to see patterns, behaviors, and emotional climates that drain you instead of building you. And if no one teaches you to recognize these patterns, you might spend years blaming yourself for what was never your fault.

This is why you must understand how narcissistic, controlling, and insecure leadership works. Not to condemn leaders, but to protect your heart, discern spiritual environments, and finally name what you experienced. Nevertheless, **some leaders are not evil. They are just unhealed. But unhealed shepherds can still bleed on sheep.**

Narcissistic leadership is not always loud. Sometimes it looks humble on the outside but empty on the inside. At its core, narcissism is a hunger for admiration, validation, and attention. It is a heart that needs to be worshipped even if it quotes scriptures. Paul warned Timothy about such leaders, *"lovers of themselves"* (2 Timothy 3:2). Notice the phrase "lovers of themselves". It means the affection that should flow outward toward the people now flows inward toward the ego.

Narcissistic leaders often preach well, but the pulpit becomes a mirror. Every sermon circles back to their greatness, their revelation, their sacrifice, and their vision. You notice the pattern: you exist to applaud them, not to grow. They love testimonies that make them look powerful. They dislike feedback that exposes their weakness. They use spiritual language to decorate insecurity. But you can feel the weight of it because spiritual leadership was never designed to be a stage for ego; it was designed to be a place of service. Jesus said plainly, "The Son of Man came not to be served, but to serve" (Matthew 20:28). Where service dies, narcissism grows.

Most times, controlling leadership is subtle at first. It feels like guidance. It sounds like wisdom. It looks like protection. But slowly, the boundaries shift. The leader begins to speak into things God did not give them jurisdiction over: your choices, your relationships, your career, your money, and even your thoughts. Before long, you start doubting your ability to hear God without them. Control works like a slow leak in a boat. It drains confidence without you noticing.

A controlling leader does not trust God to lead you. They trust themselves to lead you. They fear your independence because it threatens their power. They hide control behind phrases like "submission", "spiritual covering", or "honor", until you start living more to please them than to please God. This behavior contradicts what Peter taught leaders: "not lording it over those entrusted to you, but being examples" (1 Peter 5:3). "Lording over" means dominating, manipulating, or forcing obedience. That is not spiritual guidance. That is spiritual colonization. If a leader demands obedience instead of inspiring obedience, something is already wrong.

Then there are insecure leaders. They look bold on stage, but off stage they crumble if they are not constantly affirmed. Insecurity is a restless master. It pushes leaders to protect their image more than their people. They become threatened by gifted members. They silence anyone who shines. They reject anyone who questions. They spiritualize their insecurity and call it "discernment".

You may have seen it before: a leader reacting harshly to harmless feedback. Or preaching a whole sermon in reaction to one person. Or using prophecy to correct instead of restore. It all comes from the same place: **insecurity hates accountability.**

Saul is the perfect biblical picture of insecure leadership. He started humble, but the moment he sensed David's favor increasing, he became a threat. Instead of nurturing David, he threw spears at him. Insecurity makes a leader see sons as competitors and helpers as threats.

Do you ever wonder why some leaders must dominate? Why must they be feared to feel respected? Because dominance is the counterfeit of identity. When a leader does not know who they are in God, they will use people to feel like somebody. When they feel insignificant, they inflate themselves through exaggerated authority. When they fear abandonment, they tighten control. When they fear exposure, they silence questions.

This is why God never intended leadership to be rooted in human strength. Paul said, *"We have this treasure in jars of clay"* (2 Corinthians 4:7). The vessel is fragile, but the treasure is divine. When a leader forgets this, they start pretending to be stronger than they are, which leads to manipulation, fear, and spiritual intimidation.

Jesus washed feet. Many leaders today want their feet washed. Leadership without humility becomes tyranny. Leadership without vulnerability becomes performance. Leadership without accountability becomes abusive. When leaders isolate themselves from correction, they stop shepherding and start ruling. And rulership is not the kingdom model. Jesus made this clear: "The greatest among you will be your servant" (Matthew 23:11). The word *"servant"* in Greek, "diakonos", means "one who runs to serve". Not one who runs to control, impress, or dominate. If a leader cannot serve, they cannot lead.

You see, spiritual manipulation in the form of church abuse often starts with insecurity. A leader fears losing influence, so they exaggerate spiritual authority. They claim exclusive access to God's voice. They act as though their instruction carries the same weight as scripture. They use fear to keep people loyal. They use prophecy to assert superiority. They shame you for questioning. They subtly teach that leaving them is equal to leaving God. This is not discipleship, it is bondage and bondage grows wherever leaders are not healed.

Even though these patterns are damaging, many leaders are not intentionally malicious. They are human beings shaped by trauma, rejection, pressure, and unhealed childhood wounds. That does not excuse the harm, but it helps you understand the spiritual climate. Hurt leaders hurt people. Insecure leaders create insecure churches. Controlling leaders attract passive followers. Narcissistic leaders build empires, not families. And when you understand this, you stop internalizing the abuse. You stop blaming yourself. You stop thinking you "failed". You realize you were under a leader who needed healing they never received.

The truth remains that **you cannot heal under someone who is bleeding on you.** You cannot thrive where your identity is trimmed down to fit someone's insecurity. You cannot grow where control has replaced love. You cannot serve freely where fear is the currency of honor. The good news is that God sees. Ezekiel 34 is God's response to abusive shepherds. He said, *"I myself will search for my sheep and look after them"* (Ezekiel 34:11). God steps in when leaders fail. God gathers the wounded. God restores what was broken. God defends those who were mishandled. You are not abandoned. You are not forgotten. Your healing matters more to God than any leader's title. And He will walk you into wholeness, one truth at a time.

The Spirit behind Misused Authority

Misused authority is never just about personality, preference, or leadership style. Behind every pattern of domination, manipulation, control, or spiritual intimidation, there is always a deeper force at work, a spirit that stands in direct opposition to the character of Christ. When authority shifts from servant-hearted leadership to self-exaltation, something spiritual has already shifted. This is why abuse in spiritual spaces feels heavier than ordinary conflict; it carries a weight that goes beyond human interaction. People can sense when something about a leader's behavior is "off", even when they cannot fully articulate it. That inner alarm often signals the presence of a spirit foreign to the nature of God.

Healthy spiritual authority flows from humility, reverence for God, and a deep awareness that leadership is stewardship, not ownership. But misused authority begins when leaders slowly drift toward self-importance. They stop seeing themselves as servants and start seeing themselves as "God's special emissaries", beyond correction or accountability. The honor they once carried with reverence now becomes entitlement.

When a leader begins to believe they are irreplaceable, unquestionable, or superior, the fear of God fades. And when the fear of God fades, the door opens wide for a spirit of pride, control, and self-exaltation to operate. This is the same spirit that corrupted Lucifer; what began as beauty, gifting, and divine placement became twisted through pride into a hunger to dominate rather than serve.

You can often identify this shift in leaders who constantly remind people of their titles, demand recognition, or insist that obedience to them is equal to obedience to God. The spirit behind misused authority is always rooted in pride, because pride is the soil where spiritual manipulation grows. A leader functioning under God's Spirit guides, teaches, corrects, and nurtures with gentleness and patience. But a leader controlled by an unhealthy spirit enforces submission through fear, guilt, or intimidation. They do not simply want cooperation; they want absolute control over thoughts, choices, and movements.

This spirit manifests in subtle but destructive ways:

- Decisions must go through them, even those that are personal or family-related.

- Members are made to feel guilty for questioning anything.

- People are subtly threatened with "spiritual consequences" if they do not comply.

- The leader becomes the final authority on everything, even matters outside the church.

The result is psychological and spiritual captivity. People stay not because they feel spiritually nourished, but because they fear repercussions, fear being cursed, fear losing spiritual covering, and fear being labelled rebellious. This is not the Spirit of God. Scripture says, "Where the Spirit of the Lord is, there is liberty," which means where there is bondage, manipulation, or fear, another spirit is at work.

One of the clearest signs of spiritual manipulation is the systematic breakdown of discernment within the congregation. Healthy leaders teach people to hear God, study Scripture, and grow in spiritual maturity. Unhealthy leaders, driven by the wrong spirit, create dependency instead of discipleship. They discourage independent thinking and make congregation members believe they cannot discern God's will without the leader's interpretation.

Instead of helping believers mature, they infantilize them. They redefine obedience to God as obedience to the leader, they portray questioning as rebellion and they suppress critical thinking and mute spiritual instincts. This spirit thrives where people stop trusting their own ability to hear God. When a believer's confidence is broken, they lose the ability to challenge error, confront injustice, or even walk away from abusive authority. This is why many victims of spiritual abuse say, "I felt something was wrong, but I could not trust my own thoughts anymore." That internal confusion is the goal of the spirit behind misused authority; it blinds discernment so that deception becomes easier to maintain.

You see, misused authority is fueled by a spirit of fear, not love. Fear is the favorite weapon of abusive leadership. They use fear of divine punishment, fear of losing blessings, fear of public shame, or fear of spiritual attack to keep people caged in submission. But fear does not come from God. Scripture says, "Perfect love casts out fear." Fear is the environment in which abusive authority thrives because fear weakens identity, erodes confidence, and makes people easy to dominate.

Leaders driven by the wrong spirit weaponize spiritual language to produce fear. For instance, they can say things like:

- "If you leave this church, your life will fall apart."

- "If you question me, you are fighting God."

- "If you do not obey, something bad will happen."

These statements are not prophetic warnings; they are psychological shackles. Where fear rules, the Holy Spirit is not the one leading. God's presence brings conviction, comfort, wisdom, and freedom, not terror designed to enforce submission.

Moreover, when the spirit behind leadership shifts, the church environment begins to subtly resemble a cult, even if it still looks like a regular church. The leader becomes the center of spiritual life, the interpreter of God's will, and the controller of people's destinies. Loyalty to the leader becomes more important than loyalty to Christ.

This spirit seeks isolation: people are discouraged from relating outside the group, from listening to other pastors, or from receiving counsel elsewhere. Isolation strengthens control. The more cut off a believer is, the more dependent they become on the abusive structure. Very often, the church becomes the leader's personal kingdom rather than Christ's body. When teachings revolve more around protecting the leader's position than nurturing the people's souls, the church has shifted spiritually into dangerous territory.

Perhaps the most tragic impact of this spirit is that it corrupts how people see God. Because spiritual leaders represent God to the congregation, when their authority becomes abusive, people unconsciously attach those behaviors to God Himself. Harsh leaders create the image of a harsh God. Controlling leaders create the image of a controlling God. Proud leaders create the image of a proud, easily offended God.

This distortion damages prayer life, worship, and relationship with God. Many believers wounded under misused authority find it hard to trust God again, not because God wounded them, but because the spirit that influenced the leadership used God's name as a weapon. This misrepresentation is spiritual theft. It steals the purity of God's image from the hearts of His children.

Escaping the influence of misused authority is not merely a physical decision; it is a spiritual process. The first step is recognizing that something spiritually unhealthy is happening. Then comes the courage to reclaim your spiritual autonomy, your voice, your ability to hear God, and your identity in Christ. Healing begins when believers separate the heart of God from the behaviors of flawed leaders. It continues when they reconnect with Scripture, rebuild trust in their own discernment, and seek safe, accountable spiritual communities. The spirit behind misused authority breaks people, but the Spirit of God restores them.

Chapter Seven:

Congregations That Devour Their Own

Gossip, Slander and Spiritual Bullying Among Believers

You would think that the safest place for a believer should be the house of God. A place of warmth. A place of refuge. A place where your wounds are wrapped with prayer and tenderness. But for many people, the church has become the very place where their deepest bruises were formed. Not because demons attacked them in the night, but because the mouths of brethren cut them during the day. Gossip, slander, and spiritual bullying have turned many church environments into quiet battlegrounds where smiles hide swords and "God bless you" is sometimes just a covering for quiet hostility.

Let's begin with the word that names the problem plainly. Proverbs 18:21 says, *"Death and life are in the power of the tongue."* Notice the word power; your tongue carries the ability to build or break, uplift or undo. And James 3:6 follows like a thunderclap: *"The tongue is a fire… and sets on fire the course of nature."* A single careless sentence can set someone's destiny on fire and that is not an exaggeration. That is scripture describing what many believers have felt firsthand.

Gossip is more than "small talk". It is the practice of spreading information, true or false, without the person's consent, without their presence, and without the intention to heal. It is conversation that kills honor, kills reputation, and sometimes kills the desire to serve God. Gossip feels small until you are the one being discussed. Then you understand that it is not small at all. It is emotional pickpocketing. It steals peace, dignity, and trust.

Slander goes even deeper. It is the intentional twisting of truth to make someone look worse than they are. It paints people with colors God never approved. It adds shadows to their name. It builds false narratives that spread faster than wildfire. One person whispers it, another person adds "their own", and before long, the entire story becomes a monster the person never created. This is why the Bible is firm about it. Ephesians 4:31 commands,

> ***"Let all bitterness and wrath and anger and clamor and evil speaking be put away from you."***

God did not say, "Reduce it." He said, 'Put **it** away,' as in 'remove it like a dangerous weapon.' But spiritual bullying is one many do not talk about. It is the intimidation that hides under scriptures. The pressure that hides under "correction". The humiliation that hides under "I'm only saying this to help you." You know spiritual bullying when someone uses their position, spiritual age, or influence to make you feel small, foolish, unworthy, or less spiritual. It is correction without compassion. Advice without love. Counsel without humility. It is leadership without gentleness and fellowship without kindness.

You see this bullying in the way some believers gang up on the weak, the slow, the different, the recovering, the honest, the new, and the unsure. If someone is struggling, instead of offering a hand, some offer gossip. Instead of encouragement, they offer whispers.

Instead of help, they offer judgment. A spiritually bullied believer begins to shrink inside. They pray less, they show up less, they trust less, they speak less. And slowly, their fire begins to die, not because God is far from them, but because His people pushed them to the corner.

Jesus never bullied the weak. He never mocked the sinner. He never used someone's past as a sermon title. He never gossiped about the woman caught in adultery. He never slandered Peter when he denied Him, He restored gently. He corrected with strength but wrapped it in mercy. He always healed; He never humiliated. If your behavior wounds more than it heals, it is not Christ like, no matter how many scriptures you quote to defend it.

You know how gossip spreads? It spreads because people rarely challenge it. It spreads because it feels "light". It spreads because we treat words like feathers instead of bullets. But every rumor in the church moves with an assignment. Every false story grows legs. Every careless comment finds ears. And every unhealed heart becomes a receiver for spiritual poison disguised as "concern".

Sometimes the worst wounds come from the ones who said, "I'm praying for you." Sometimes the deepest pain comes from people who clap during worship and sling words during fellowship. This is why the Bible warns us again and again to guard our mouths and guard our unity. Gossip is not harmless. Slander is not harmless. Spiritual bullying is not harmless. These things tear the fabric of a church from the inside.

Think of it like termites. Termites are tiny, they do not roar, they do not bite loudly, they just nibble silently until the beams supporting the house collapse. Gossip does the same thing. It nibbles at fellowship. It weakens trust. It hollows out relationships. And before long, a congregation becomes a group of suspicious people smiling through guarded hearts.

Maybe you have been on the receiving end. Maybe you walked into church and felt eyes scanning you. Maybe your story was told without your permission. Maybe you were reduced to a rumor. Maybe you were spiritually bullied for not praying loud enough, not dressing "holy" enough, or not conforming quickly enough. If that is you, hear me: God sees you. God defends you. And God will heal you. You are not the problem. Their words were the problem. Their behavior was not a reflection of God's heart. It was a reflection of their own unhealed places.

But maybe you have also been on the giving end. Maybe you have carried information that wasn't yours to carry. Maybe you have amplified a story instead of shutting it down. Maybe you laughed at a rumor because it wasn't "serious". Maybe you joined a group conversation that felt harmless. If so, this is not condemnation. This is a gentle warning. Stop before your words become someone's wound. Stop before you become an unknowing tool the devil uses to injure a brother or sister Christ died for.

God calls us to speak life. To be healers with our tongues. To be defenders, not destroyers. To be safe company, not dangerous company. He calls us to create atmospheres where people can breathe, grow, learn, and rise without being afraid of becoming the next discussion topic. This is how we build a church that looks like Christ. This is how we protect fragile hearts. This is how we ensure that our fellowship becomes a garden, not a battlefield. Whenever you open your mouth, remember this simple truth: your words are seeds. Be intentional in choosing what you plant.

How Competition and Jealousy Create Toxic Atmospheres

Competition did not begin in heaven, but jealousy did. And when jealousy walked into heaven, it was cast out. That alone should tell you something. There is nothing holy about competition when it replaces love, unity, and honor in the body of Christ. Yet many church spaces are quietly soaked in rivalry, comparison, and silent contests that no one openly names, but everyone feels. It is the tension in the room. The cold smiles. The subtle pulling away. The unspoken pressure to "measure up".

The Bible is clear and unapologetic. James 3:16 says,

"For where envy and self-seeking exist, confusion and every evil thing are there."

Notice the word **confusion**. Toxic church atmospheres do not start loud. They start confused. Confused motives. Confused loyalties. Confused identities. When competition enters the house of God, clarity exits. Peace leaks out. Unity fractures quietly.

Competition becomes especially dangerous in church because it is often baptized with spiritual language. It is not called envy. It is called "zeal". It is not called insecurity. It is called "passion for God". It is not called comparison. It is called "pushing for excellence". But underneath those polished words, something rotten can grow. You begin to see believers sizing each other up. Who is more anointed? Who is more visible? Who sings better? Who prays louder? Who serves closer to leadership. Who is recognized or overlooked. This is what some people call "holy competition". But there is nothing holy about it. Heaven does not compete. Heaven complements. When Paul wrote to the Corinthians, he addressed this exact issue.

"For you are still carnal. For where there are envy, strife, and divisions among you, are you not carnal?"

(1 Corinthians 3:3).

Paul did not excuse envy as maturity. He called it carnality. Flesh. Human insecurity dressed up in church clothes. Competition is not a sign of spiritual growth. It is a sign that identity is still under construction.

Jealousy begins when you forget who you are. It grows when you measure your calling with someone else's assignment. It matures when you start resenting the grace in another person's life. And it becomes toxic when it turns into silent hostility, subtle sabotage, or emotional withdrawal. People stop clapping genuinely. They stop celebrating others. They stop praying clean prayers. Everything becomes filtered through comparison. Comparison is a thief. It steals joy. It steals gratitude. It steals contentment. And in the church, it steals unity.

You see it when someone's success makes the room uncomfortable. You see it when promotion creates distance instead of celebration. You see it when someone's gift is minimized because it threatens another's relevance. Instead of saying, "God did it," jealousy whispers, "Why not me?" Instead of saying, "There is room for all of us," competition says, "Only one can shine." That mindset does not come from the Spirit of Christ. It comes from scarcity thinking, not kingdom thinking.

The kingdom of God is not a stage with limited microphones. It is a body with many parts. Romans 12:4–5 reminds us,

"For as we have many members in one body, but all the members do not have the same function… so we, being many, are one body in Christ."

When one part competes with another, the body injures itself. Imagine your eye competing with your hand. Imagine your heart resenting your lungs. It sounds ridiculous, yet that is what jealousy does in the church. And who suffers the most? The vulnerable, new believers, quiet believers, those still healing and those finding their voice. They walk into an atmosphere thick with comparison and do not know why they suddenly feel small. They do not know why serving now feels stressful instead of joyful. They do not know why they are afraid to grow or shine. Rivalries crush them before they even understand what is happening. They either shrink to survive or leave to breathe.

Jealousy rarely confronts openly. It works through coldness. Through exclusion. Through backhanded compliments. Through silence where support should be. Through spiritual pride disguised as discernment. Someone says, "I do not feel peace about them," when what they really feel is threatened. Someone says, "They are too much," when what they really mean is, "They are getting attention." This is how competition poisons fellowship. It turns brothers into rivals, sisters into silent enemies, teams into territories, and ministries into brands. Suddenly, the church becomes a marketplace instead of a family.

Jesus addressed this spirit directly when His disciples argued about who was the greatest. He did not applaud their ambition. He corrected their mindset.

"Whoever desires to become great among you, let him be your servant."

(Matthew 20:26).

In God's kingdom, greatness is not proven by visibility but by humility. Not by dominance, but by service. Not by outshining others, but by lifting them. Jealousy cannot survive where love is practiced intentionally. Love celebrates without envy. Love honors without comparison. Love creates room. Love says, "If God blesses you, it does not reduce me." That is maturity. That is freedom. If you sense jealousy rising in your heart, do not condemn yourself. Pause and ask honest questions. Why does this trigger me? What insecurity is being exposed? What lie about myself am I believing? Healing begins when you stop pretending and start confronting the root. And if you have been crushed by someone else's jealousy, hear this clearly: their behavior is not proof that you are wrong; it is proof that you carry something valuable. Do not dim your light to make insecure people comfortable. God did not anoint you to shrink. He anointed you to serve, to grow, to shine in your lane.

The church becomes toxic when competition replaces communion. But it becomes healing again when believers learn to rejoice with those who rejoice, weep with those who weep, and walk side by side without measuring worth by visibility. This is the kind of house God is restoring. A house without rivalry, without comparison and a house where love outgrows jealousy. And you get to be part of that healing.

Chapter Eight:

The Spirit Realm Behind Church Abuse

Spiritual Strongholds Operating In Abusive Environments

Church abuse does not survive on human behavior alone. It feeds on something deeper, darker, and often unseen. Behind repeated patterns of control, fear, silence, and manipulation, there is usually a **spiritual stronghold** holding the environment hostage. Until that stronghold is confronted, named, and broken, abuse will keep recycling itself, changing faces, changing voices, but keeping the same spirit. The Bible gives us language for this.

> *"For the weapons of our warfare are not carnal, but mighty through God to the pulling down of strongholds"*

> *(2 Corinthians 10:4).*

The word **'stronghold'** here comes from the Greek 'ochyrōma', meaning a fortified place, a prison, or a mindset that resists truth. A stronghold is not always dramatic. Sometimes it looks spiritual. Sometimes it sounds biblical. But it always resists freedom.

Strongholds thrive where sin goes unchallenged and pride is protected. When leaders are never corrected, when accountability is silenced, when "honor" becomes an excuse for secrecy, the atmosphere becomes fertile ground for spiritual oppression. Abuse it does not just happen because people are flawed. It happens because darkness has been given permission to stay.

Pride is often the front door. Pride says, "I cannot be questioned." Pride says, "I hear God more than others." Pride says, "My position excuses my behavior." And where pride settles comfortably, God's presence quietly withdraws. Scripture is blunt about this: *"God resists the proud, but gives grace to the humble"* (James 4:6). If God is resisting something, you can be sure something else is empowering it.

One of the clearest signs of a stronghold-driven church culture is **repetition**. The same issues keep resurfacing. Different victims, same wounds. Different leaders, same abuse patterns. People leave hurt, but nothing changes. Apologies are made, but repentance never follows. That cycle is not accidental, it is spiritual.

Another sign is **normalized dysfunction**. People learn to live with things that should alarm them. Harsh leadership becomes "strong leadership". Fear-based teaching becomes "deep revelation". Emotional manipulation becomes "spiritual discipline". Over time, the atmosphere numbs discernment. What once felt wrong now feels familiar. That is how strongholds survive, by making bondage feel normal.

Strongholds also thrive on **silence**. When people are afraid to speak, afraid to ask questions, and afraid to say, "This does not feel right," the stronghold tightens its grip. Silence is not neutral. Silence protects darkness. Abuse grows best where people are spiritually threatened into quietness. This is why victims often say, "I knew something was wrong, but I did not know how to say it." Jesus never created fear-filled silence around Himself. People questioned Him openly. Even His enemies spoke. Truth was never hidden behind intimidation. So when a church environment punishes honest questions, something is spiritually off.

Strongholds blind **both leaders and members**. Leaders begin to believe their own narratives. They stop self-reflecting. They stop listening. Correction feels like an attack. Accountability feels like rebellion. Members, on the other hand, lose clarity. They second-guess their instincts. They spiritualize discomfort. They call oppression "process". They confuse endurance with holiness.

This blindness is dangerous. Jesus warned about it clearly: *"If the blind lead the blind, both will fall into a ditch"* (Matthew 15:14). Strongholds do not just hurt individuals. They endanger entire communities.

Another pattern is **selective spirituality**. Scripture is quoted, but only the parts that protect power. Prophecy flows, but only toward control. Prayer is encouraged, but discernment is discouraged. The Bible is used as a tool instead of a mirror. This is how strongholds wear religious clothing.

You will also notice **spiritual exhaustion** in stronghold-driven environments. People are always tired but never resting. Always serving but never healing. Always repenting but never free. Always confessing but never restored. This is because strongholds drain life. Jesus said, *"I have come that they may have life and have it abundantly"* (John 10:10). Where life is consistently missing, something is stealing.

Strongholds operate through agreement. Not just demonic agreement, but human agreement. When people keep excusing abuse, keep justifying wrong, and keep explaining away pain, they unknowingly strengthen the prison holding them. This is not blame. It is awareness. Freedom begins when agreement breaks.

The good news is this: strongholds are not permanent. They are not invincible. They collapse when truth enters boldly. When humility returns. When repentance becomes real. When light is allowed to shine. God is not intimidated by long-standing dysfunction. He is not impressed by religious appearance. He is drawn to honesty.

If you have lived in such an environment, hear this clearly: your confusion was not weakness. Your exhaustion was not laziness. Your inner alarm was discernment trying to survive under pressure. God saw you. God still sees you. And if you are part of a church culture that shows these patterns, this is not a call to panic; it is a call to awakening because strongholds lose power when truth is spoken with courage and love, when repentance replaces image management, when leaders return to humility and when people stop pretending.

Serpentine and Manipulative Influences Masquerading As Spiritual Gifts

Not everything that sounds spiritual comes from the Spirit of God. That sentence alone can unsettle people, but it must be said plainly. The church is not only a place of genuine gifts and divine flow. It can also become a stage where manipulation dresses itself in spiritual language and performs convincingly. The enemy rarely walks in wearing horns. As a matter of fact, He often prefers a robe, a microphone, and the right vocabulary. Scripture warns us clearly.

"For Satan himself masquerades as an angel of light"

(2 Corinthians 11:14).

The danger is not obvious darkness. The danger is **counterfeit light**. It looks close enough to confuse you. It sounds close enough to convince you. It feels spiritual enough to silence your questions.

Serpentine influence is subtle. The serpent in Genesis did not deny God outright. He twisted God's words just enough to create doubt, fear, and control. That same pattern shows up today. Manipulative influences rarely say, "God did not say." They say, "God said... but let me explain what He really meant." And suddenly, God's voice is filtered through a human agenda.

One of the clearest places manipulation hides is behind **prophetic language**. Prophecy is a real and beautiful gift. But counterfeit prophecy uses revelation as leverage. It tells you what God "showed" someone about you, your future, your danger, or your disobedience, without inviting confirmation, prayer, or peace. It creates dependency instead of maturity.

True prophecy points you back to God. Manipulative prophecy points you back to the prophet. Paul gives us a grounding test: *"The spirits of the prophets are subject to the prophets" (1 Corinthians 14:32).* In simple terms, the Holy Spirit does not hijack people. He does not override self-control. He does not force compliance. If someone claims, "I could not help it; God told me," yet their words crush, intimidate, or control, something is wrong.

Manipulation often hides behind **visions and revelations**. "I saw something about you." "God showed me something concerning your loyalty." "I had a dream about your rebellion." These statements sound powerful, but they are often used to bypass conversation and shut down discernment. Once someone claims divine access, questioning them feels like questioning God Himself and that is the trap.

The Bible never tells you to surrender your discernment to someone else's revelation. *"Beloved, do not believe every spirit, but test the spirits, whether they are of God"* (1 John 4:1). Testing is not rebellion. Testing is obedience. God expects you to weigh, discern, and confirm spiritual input, not swallow it whole because it was delivered confidently.

Serpentine influence thrives on **fear**. Fear of missing God. Fear of judgment. Fear of exposure. Fear of being labelled rebellious. Fear keeps people compliant. Love invites growth. Scripture says plainly, *"Perfect love casts out fear"* (1 John 4:18). If a spiritual environment is saturated with fear, something other than God's love is at work.

Another red flag is **private revelations used publicly**. Someone claims insight about your heart, motives, or future without your consent and uses it to shape how others see you. This is spiritual bullying disguised as discernment. Jesus corrected privately. He restored gently. He never exposed people to control them.

Manipulative influence also disguises itself as **hyper-discernment**. Everything is a demon. Every disagreement is witchcraft. Every question is rebellion. This mindset keeps people anxious and dependent. It creates a spiritual atmosphere where suspicion replaces love and paranoia replaces peace. That is not spiritual maturity. That is spiritual intimidation.

The Holy Spirit brings clarity, conviction, and comfort, even when He corrects. Manipulative spirits bring confusion, condemnation, and pressure. Paul said, *"God is not the author of confusion, but of peace"* (1 Corinthians 14:33). Confusion that lingers, disorients, and disempowers is not holy.

Let's talk about control masked as **submission**. Biblical submission is mutual, loving, and grounded in truth. Manipulative submission demands silence, agreement, and unquestioned loyalty. It teaches you that obedience to a leader equals obedience to God and that is a dangerous ground. No human occupies that position. Peter himself warned leaders not to do this:

"Not as being lords over those entrusted to you, but being examples to the flock"

(1 Peter 5:3).

When leadership becomes lordship, when guidance becomes domination, when covering becomes captivity, the spirit behind it is not Christ like.

Manipulative influence also isolates people. It subtly cuts off external voices. "They do not understand your calling." "They are jealous of what God is doing here." "Do not listen to outsiders." Isolation weakens discernment. God places believers in the body, not in cages. Genuine spiritual flow produces fruit. Love. Joy. Peace. Patience. Growth. Freedom. Counterfeit flow produces anxiety, dependence, fear, and silence. Jesus said, *"By their fruits you will know them"* (Matthew 7:16). Not by their volume. Not by their charisma. Not by their titles.

If you have ever felt spiritually pressured, emotionally confused, or inwardly disturbed while being told it was "God", pause here. You are not crazy. Your spirit was responding to misalignment. Discernment often speaks as discomfort before it speaks as clarity. The goal of this chapter is not to make you suspicious of spiritual gifts. It is to help you **recognize the difference between divine flow and deceptive influence**. God is not threatened by your discernment. He gave it to you.

Beloved, you are allowed to ask questions. You are allowed to test words. You are allowed to walk away from manipulation. God does not trap His children. He leads them. This awareness does not weaken your faith, but it strengthens it. When manipulation is exposed, genuine spirituality becomes safer, purer, and more powerful. And light always exposes the serpent, no matter how spiritual it sounds.

Chapter Nine:

Escaping The Prison Of Fear And Guilt

Healing From Fear-Based Teachings

Fear is a powerful prison. It locks doors from the inside. Many believers did not walk away from God because they loved sin. They walked away because the God they were taught to fear never felt safe to love. Somewhere along the line, faith became survival. Obedience became anxiety. And worship felt like walking on broken glass, hoping not to bleed.

Fear-based teachings often present God as short-tempered, easily offended, and constantly watching for mistakes. One wrong step and punishment follows. One doubt and judgment falls. This version of God keeps people compliant but never healed. It produces outward obedience and inward terror. Yet Scripture paints a very different picture.

"There is no fear in love; but perfect love casts out fear, because fear involves torment"

(1 John 4:18).

That word **'torment'** matters. God never uses torment to shape His children. Fear that torments is not holy fear. It is bondage wearing religious clothing.

Many doctrines lean heavily on punishment without balance. They speak often of hell, wrath, and judgment, but rarely of mercy, patience, and kindness. Truth becomes distorted when one side of God's nature is magnified and the other is buried. Yes, God is holy. But holiness without love becomes terror. Justice without mercy becomes cruelty.

The Bible says, *"The goodness of God leads you to repentance"* (Romans 2:4). Not fear, not threats, not intimidation. Repentance flows from safety. When you feel safe with God, your heart opens. When you feel hunted, your heart hides. Fear damages trust. And trust is the foundation of every healthy relationship, especially your relationship with God. If you believe God is waiting to punish you, you will approach Him guarded. You will pray cautiously. You will confess selectively. You will hide parts of yourself instead of being transformed. Adam did the same thing. After sin entered, he hid. When God asked why, Adam said, *"I was afraid"* (Genesis 3:10). Fear always leads to hiding. God came looking, not to destroy Adam, but to restore relationship. Even in correction, God moved toward him, not away.

Fear-based teachings also shape how you hear God's voice. Conviction becomes condemnation. Guidance becomes a threat. Correction feels like rejection. Over time, you begin to associate God's presence with anxiety instead of peace. That is not spiritual maturity. That is trauma. Jesus never taught this way. Look at how He treated broken people. The woman caught in adultery expected stones. Jesus offered dignity. *"Neither do I condemn you. Go and sin no more"* (John 8:11). Notice the order. No condemnation first. Transformation second. Fear was removed before change was required.

Jesus described Himself clearly: *"Come to Me, all you who labor and are heavy laden, and I will give you rest… for I am gentle and lowly in heart"* (Matthew 11:28–29). Gentle. Lowly. Rest-giving. Tyrants do not invite rest. Abusers do not lead with gentleness. Fear-based teachings often confuse **reverence** with terror. Biblical fear of the Lord is not panic. The Hebrew word *'yirah'* includes awe, honor, and deep respect. It is the fear a child has of disappointing a loving parent, not the fear of being beaten. Reverence draws you closer. Terror pushes you away.

When fear dominates your faith, shame soon follows. You start to believe something is wrong with you at your core. You do not just say, "I made a mistake." You think, "I am a mistake." Shame whispers that God tolerates you at best. That lie keeps people stuck.

But Scripture says, *"As far as the east is from the west, so far has He removed our transgressions from us"* (Psalm 103:12). God does not recycle forgiven sins. He does not rehearse your past to control your present. He heals thoroughly. Fear also affects how communities function. Fearful believers police each other. They measure spirituality by behavior. They whisper instead of restore, they judge instead of heal, but love builds safe spaces where growth happens naturally. You may need to grieve the version of God you were taught. That is okay. God is not offended when you let go of false images of Him. He is relieved. Healing begins when lies lose their power.

Start here: Separate God's voice from the voices that wounded you. God's voice convicts without crushing. It corrects without humiliating. It leads without threatening. *"My sheep hear My voice… and they follow Me"* (John 10:27). His voice produces peace, even when it challenges you. Picture God as a skilled physician, not an angry judge. Surgeons cut to heal, not to harm. God exposes wounds to restore life, not to shame you for bleeding. When fear tells you to run, God invites you to stay.

Healing from fear-based teachings takes time. Your nervous system may need to learn safety again. Prayer may feel awkward at first. Silence may feel loud. That does not mean God is distant. It means your heart is relearning trust. You are not weak for struggling. You are waking up. God is not pacing heaven with a checklist of your failures. He is walking with you, step by step, teaching you how to rest in love. Fear kept you alive once. Love will now make you whole. Breathe again. You are not in danger with God, you are home. When fear loses its grip, worship becomes joy. Obedience becomes desire. Faith becomes a relationship again. And the prison door you thought was locked was never locked at all. Love has the key.

Breaking the Chains Of Religious Manipulation

Religious manipulation is subtle. It rarely announces itself. It creeps in quietly, wearing the language of devotion, loyalty, and "spiritual maturity". Before you know it, your faith is no longer led by love but managed by fear. You still attend. You still serve. You still believe. But somewhere inside, your will has been hijacked. Manipulation thrives where spiritual dependency is encouraged. You are taught, directly or indirectly, that you cannot hear God clearly on your own. That your discernment is dangerous. That questioning is rebellion. That safety lies in submission to a system, not in intimacy with Christ.

Yet Scripture says, *"You have an anointing from the Holy One, and you all know"* (1 John 2:20). God did not design you to outsource your conscience. He gave you His Spirit so you could walk with Him personally. Any system that removes your ability to think, pray, and discern freely is not protecting your faith. It is controlling it.

One common tactic of manipulation is **spiritual fear placement**. You are warned of dire consequences if you step out of line. Covering will be removed. Protection will lift. God's favor will disappear. These threats may not be spoken boldly, but they are implied. And fear does the rest of the work. But the Bible says, *"The Lord is my shepherd; I shall not want"* (Psalm 23:1). God does not subcontract shepherding to control your life. Leaders guide. God shepherds. When a human voice replaces God's voice in your decisions, something has gone wrong.

Another tactic is **guilt-based control**. You are made to feel constantly indebted. "After all we've done for you." "Look at how much we invested in you." Gratitude is turned into obligation, service becomes repayment, and leaving feels like betrayal. But Jesus said, *"Freely you have received; freely give"* (Matthew 10:8). The kingdom is not a loan system. Grace is not a debt trap. Anything given in love should not become a leash.

Guilt manipulates behavior by attacking identity. Instead of addressing actions, it labels the person. You are called ungrateful, unteachable, proud, or rebellious. Over time, you begin to internalize these labels. You start policing yourself. You silence questions before they form. You shrink. That is not conviction. Conviction points to change. Guilt points to shame. Scripture says, *"Godly sorrow brings repentance that leads to salvation and leaves no regret"* (2 Corinthians 7:10). Manipulative guilt leaves regret, fear, and paralysis. It does not lead to life.

Another chain is **information control**. You are discouraged from reading outside materials. Testimonies that challenge the system are labelled "bitter". Stories of abuse are dismissed as attacks. Only approved narratives are allowed. Truth becomes filtered. Yet Scripture commands, *"Test all things; hold fast what is good"* (1 Thessalonians 5:21). Testing is biblical. Blind acceptance is not. Truth does not fear investigation. Lies do.

Religious manipulation also thrives on **over-spiritualizing normal human boundaries**. Wanting rest is called laziness, needing space is labelled an offence, and asking questions is framed as pride. Healthy human needs are spiritualized into sins. Jesus never did this. He withdrew to rest. He asked questions. He honored boundaries. When He was tired, He slept. When He was overwhelmed, He prayed alone. He did not confuse humanity with weakness.

Breaking free begins with recognizing these patterns without shame. You were not foolish. You were faithful. Manipulation preys on sincere hearts, not rebellious ones. Your desire to please God was used against you. That does not make you weak, it makes you human. The chains begin to loosen when you reclaim **personal spiritual agency**. This means you take responsibility for your walk with God again. You pray without fear. You read Scripture without someone else's voice hovering over your thoughts. You ask the Holy Spirit questions and trust Him to answer.

Jesus promised, *"When He, the Spirit of truth, has come, He will guide you into all truth"* (John 16:13). Not intimidate you, not to confuse you, but to guide you. Guidance assumes movement, not paralysis. You may feel disoriented at first, which is normal. When chains fall off, muscles that were unused need to strengthen. Decision-making may feel scary. Silence may feel loud. But freedom always feels unfamiliar before it feels safe.

Another step is **renaming God correctly**. Manipulation often attaches God's name to human control. Separate them. God is not manipulative. God is not coercive. God does not rule by fear. Scripture says, *"Where the Spirit of the Lord is, there is liberty"* (2 Corinthians 3:17). Liberty is God's atmosphere. You are allowed to say no. You are allowed to rest. You are allowed to ask questions. You are allowed to grow beyond spaces that once helped you. Growth does not dishonor God. Stagnation does. Some chains fall quickly. Others loosen slowly. Be patient with yourself. Healing is not rebellion. Distance is not backsliding. Boundaries are not bitterness. Sometimes stepping away is obedience.

God is not threatened by your freedom. He designed it. Can you imagine Lazarus walking out of the tomb? Jesus raised him, but others had to unwrap him. *"Loose him, and let him go"* (John 11:44). Resurrection came first. Unwrapping followed. You may be alive again spiritually but still shedding grave clothes. That is okay. You are not leaving God, instead, you are leaving control. You are not losing faith; instead, you are reclaiming it. Fear and guilt once kept you compliant. Love will now keep you anchored. The chains were never holy. And the freedom ahead is not dangerous. It is necessary, so walk forward. You are not alone because God is walking with you, without chains in His hands.

Chapter Ten:

Meeting God Outside The Noise

How God Visits the Wounded Personally

When the noise stops, many people panic. Silence feels unsafe at first. You were trained to believe that God only speaks loudly, through crowds, systems, and constant activity. So when you step away from the chaos, you wonder if you have stepped away from God Himself. But Scripture tells a different story. God often does His deepest work away from the noise. From Genesis to Revelation, God has a pattern. When someone is wounded, confused, rejected, or overwhelmed, he does not shout over the chaos. He draws them aside, He meets them personally. Quietly, intimately and on purpose.

Do you remember Hagar? She was used, discarded and sent away with little explanation. She found herself alone in the wilderness, pregnant, afraid, and invisible to people. Yet that was where God met her.

"The angel of the Lord found Hagar near a spring in the desert"

(Genesis 16:7).

Not in Abraham's camp. Not in Sarah's tent. In the wilderness. God saw her there. She called Him **El Roi**, meaning "the God who sees me" (Genesis 16:13). Not the God who controls me. Not the God who shames me. The God who sees me. You may feel unseen by people right now. Misunderstood. Forgotten. But God has not lost sight of you. He never meets the wounded with accusation. He meets them with recognition.

Elijah knew this too; after standing boldly against false prophets, he collapsed under fear and exhaustion. He ran into the wilderness and asked God to take his life. Burnout had swallowed his courage. What did God do? He did not rebuke him. He fed him and let him sleep, twice. Then He spoke, and when God finally addressed Elijah, it was not in the wind, earthquake, or fire. It was in a still, small voice (1 Kings 19:12). God waited for the noise to pass before He spoke clearly. This matters because when you are wounded, your soul cannot hear through chaos. God knows this. That is why He often removes you from loud places before He restores you. Jesus followed this pattern constantly. When crowds pressed Him, He withdrew. When disciples misunderstood Him, He prayed alone. When grief hit hard after John the Baptist's death, He stepped away to be with the Father (Matthew 14:13). If Jesus needed quiet to process pain, you are not weak for needing it too. One of the enemy's greatest lies is that isolation equals abandonment. Scripture disagrees.

"The Lord is near to the brokenhearted and saves those who are crushed in spirit"

(Psalm 34:18).

Near does not always look busy. Near often looks gentle. God's nearness brings three things when He meets the wounded: **comfort, clarity, and direction.** Comfort comes first. Always. God does not rush healing. He tends wounds before giving instructions. David said, *"He restores my soul"* (Psalm 23:3). Restoration is slow work, like setting a broken bone; it requires stillness. Many believers struggle here because they are used to performance-based spirituality. Do more, pray harder, serve faster. But wounded souls need rest, not pressure. God knows when you are bleeding. He does not demand speed from the injured.

Clarity comes next. When the noise fades, lies lose their grip. You start to see what was normalized but never healthy. You recognize manipulation without needing to demonize yourself. Light enters gently. Jesus said,

"You shall know the truth, and the truth shall make you free"

(John 8:32).

Freedom begins with seeing clearly. And clarity rarely comes in crowded, controlling environments. It comes when you are finally allowed to breathe.

Direction is the last gift in the set. God does not confuse healing with hiding. Seasons of stepping away are not permanent exile. They are recalibration. God speaks about next steps only after the heart is safe again. Take a look at Moses. He fled Egypt as a failure and spent forty years in obscurity. But it was there, in tending sheep, far from power, that God spoke from the burning bush (Exodus 3). Moses did not lose his calling in isolation. He found clarity there. This is important for you to hear: stepping away from abusive noise does not cancel destiny. It protects it.

Many wounded believers fear that isolation means spiritual danger. But Scripture shows that God often protects His children by pulling them aside. Jesus Himself was led by the Spirit into the wilderness (Luke 4:1). Not by disobedience, but by divine direction. The wilderness is not punishment, it is preparation. You may feel lonely, but you are not alone. God often does His most personal conversations one-on-one; no audience, no pressure, no comparison. This is where trust is rebuilt. Slowly and Tenderly.

Trust grows when you realize God does not speak like your abusers. He does not rush you. He does not threaten you. He does not confuse obedience with silence. His voice brings peace, even when it challenges you. Isaiah 30:21 says, *"You will hear a voice behind you, saying, 'This is the way; walk in it.'"* Not shouting, not shaming, but guiding.

In quiet seasons, God separates His voice from every other voice that shaped you. You begin to recognize tone again. God's tone heals. It does not dominate. Some days, God will speak clearly. Other days, He will simply sit with you. Both are sacred. Healing does not require constant revelation. Sometimes presence is enough. You are allowed to rest without explanation. You are allowed to heal without apology. You are allowed to trust that God is near, even when life is quiet.

The noise lied to you. God never needed it. He is not lost without the crowd. He is not distant without the system. He is not silent because you stepped away. He is closer than ever and He is speaking, softly, personally, faithfully, to the wounded child He has never stopped seeing.

How Wilderness Seasons Restore Spiritual Identity

The wilderness has a bad reputation. It is often described as empty, harsh, and unwanted. Yet in Scripture, the wilderness is one of God's favorite classrooms. Not to punish or to discard, but to restore identity. When everything familiar falls away, what remains is who you really are. Many believers enter wilderness seasons after church wounds, spiritual abuse, or deep disappointment. Suddenly, the titles drop. The platforms disappear. The expectations fade. And what rises is a frightening question: *who am I without all of that?* God answers that question gently.

Israel's wilderness journey was not random. God delivered them from Egypt in one night, but He took forty years to deliver Egypt out of them. Slavery had shaped their thinking. They knew how to obey orders but not how to trust love. The wilderness became the place where God reintroduced Himself, not as a taskmaster, but as a provider.

"I carried you on eagles' wings and brought you to Myself"

(Exodus 19:4).

Notice the language. God did not say, "I brought you to a system." He said, "I brought you to Myself."

That is what wilderness seasons do; they strip away substitutes so relationships can be rebuilt. Spiritual identity is not about what you do for God. It is about who you are with Him. Yet abusive environments often reverse this. You were valued for output, loyalty, silence, or endurance. Over time, your worth became performance-based. The wilderness breaks that lie. Jesus entered the wilderness before He began public ministry. Before miracles. Before crowds. Before the cross. And the very first attack He faced targeted identity: *"If you are the Son of God..."* (Matthew 4:3). The enemy always challenges identity in quiet places. But Jesus did not argue. He did not prove Himself. He rested in what the Father had already spoken: *"This is my beloved Son"* (Matthew 3:17). That is the order; identity before activity. In the wilderness, God restores that order for you.

Silence plays a big role here. Silence is uncomfortable because it removes distractions. It exposes inner noise. Old fears, old beliefs, old voices. But silence is also healing, it allows you to hear God without distortion. Psalm 46:10 says, *"Be still, and know that I am God."* Stillness is not inactivity. It is attentiveness. It is choosing to stop striving so truth can settle.

Many people fear silence because it feels like loss. But silence is not emptiness, it is space; space for God to speak without competition, space for your soul to exhale.

In the wilderness, God often replaces borrowed identity with rooted identity. You stop defining yourself by church approval, spiritual performance, or leader affirmation. You begin to define yourself by sonship and belonging. Romans 8:15 says,

"You did not receive the spirit of bondage again to fear, but you received the Spirit of adoption."

Adoption means security. Not conditional acceptance. Not fear-driven obedience. Belonging. This shift changes everything. You stop asking, "Am I enough?" You start knowing, "I am loved." You stop chasing validation. You start walking in quiet confidence. This restoration is slow, intentional and gentle.

Moses spent forty years in the wilderness after forty years in Pharaoh's palace. God had to undo identity shaped by power before He could entrust him with leadership. Shepherding sheep prepared him to shepherd people. Obscurity refined him. Silence humbled him. Time healed him. By the time God called him again, Moses no longer relied on position. He relied on presence. Wilderness seasons also heal your relationship with God's voice. In abusive systems, God's voice may have been confused with human control. Commands replaced compassion. Fear replaced freedom. Over time, discernment dulled. In the wilderness, God teaches you to atone again.

Jesus said, *"My sheep hear My voice, and I know them, and they follow Me"* (John 10:27). His voice carries safety. It does not rush. It does not threaten. It does not confuse. You begin to recognize when God is speaking versus when fear is speaking. You learn that conviction brings hope, not shame. Correction brings clarity, not dread. Identity heals when trust is rebuilt.

Another powerful gift of the wilderness is permission to feel. Many wounded believers were taught to suppress emotion. Doubt was rebellion. Pain was weakness. Questions were sin. But God never demanded emotional numbness. The Psalms are full of honest cries. Confusion, anger, tears, longing. God did not silence David. He preserved his prayers. The wilderness gives you permission to grieve what you lost without guilt. Lost trust. Lost community. Lost years. Grief is not ingratitude. It is honesty.

The book of Isaiah 61:3 says God gives *"beauty for* ashes". Ashes come from what burnt down. God does not deny the fire. He transforms the remains. Over time, something remarkable happens. You stop trying to get back to who you were. You begin becoming who you were always meant to be. The wilderness does not erase calling. It purifies it. You return without fear-driven loyalty. Without people-pleasing. Without spiritual anxiety. You return with boundaries. With discernment. With humility. With peace. Or sometimes, you do not return to the same place at all. And that is okay too. God's goal is not relocation. It is restoration. Hosea 2:14 says, *"I will allure her, bring her into the wilderness, and speak tenderly to her."* Tenderly. That is God's heart. Not harsh. Not loud. Tender. If you are in a wilderness season, do not rush it, do not fight it, and do not label it failure.

It is sacred ground. God is rebuilding you from the inside out. Not for applause or approval, But for freedom. And when identity is restored, nothing can control you the same way again. You will know who you are. You will know whose you are. And you will walk forward, whole, healed, and anchored in truth.

Chapter Eleven:

Finding Rest For The Wounded Soul

The Journey from Bitterness to Peace

Bitterness rarely announces itself loudly. It slips in quietly, like dust settling on furniture you once polished with joy. It begins as disappointment, then hurt. Then anger that stays too long. Before you know it, something hard forms around your heart, not because you are evil, but because you were wounded and never given space to heal. Church betrayal cuts deep because it happens in a place meant to be safe. You trusted, you served, and you opened your heart. What you received in return was rejection, silence, control, or misuse. That kind of pain does not disappear with prayer clichés. It lingers. It asks questions. It demands honesty.

Jesus understands betrayal deeply. He was wounded by those closest to Him. A disciple sold Him. A friend denied Him. Religious leaders misrepresented God while condemning Him. So when Scripture speaks about bitterness, it does not speak from a distance. Hebrews 12:15 warns,

> *"See to it that no root of bitterness springs up and causes trouble, and by it many become defiled."*

Notice the word *root*. Bitterness grows underground first. You may still smile. Still worship. Still functioning. But inside, something is tightening.

The journey to peace does not begin by pretending you are fine. It begins by naming the wound. Many wounded believers feel guilty for their anger. You may have been told that anger equals sin. But Scripture makes room for righteous emotion. Ephesians 4:26 says, *"Be angry, and do not sin."* Anger itself is not the enemy. Unprocessed anger is. Betrayal produces anger because something precious was violated. Trust was broken. Boundaries were crossed. Your spirit recognized injustice even when your mouth stayed silent. God does not shame you for feeling this way. He invites you to bring it to Him. The Psalms are full of raw emotion. David did not sanitize his prayers; He cried, he complained, he asked hard questions. Yet God called him a man after His heart. Why? Because honesty keeps the heart soft.

Peace does not come by suppressing pain. It comes by processing it in God's presence. Bitterness forms when pain has nowhere to go. When you are not allowed to speak. When your story is dismissed. When your tears are spiritualized away. Over time, the heart builds walls for protection. Those walls feel safe, but they also block peace. Jesus invites you into a different posture.

"Come to Me, all you who labor and are heavy laden, and I will give you rest" (Matthew 11:28). Rest is not the absence of pain. It is the presence of safety.

The Greek word for 'rest' here is 'anapausis', meaning relief, refreshment, or a pause that restores strength. Jesus does not rush you. He does not pressure you. He carries what you can no longer hold. Releasing anger does not mean denying what happened. It means choosing not to let what happened define you.

Forgiveness is often misunderstood. It is not reconciliation without repentance. It is not returning to unsafe spaces. It is not excusing abuse. Forgiveness is releasing your right to revenge and trusting God with justice. Romans 12:19 says, *"Vengeance is Mine; I will repay, says the Lord."* That verse is not passive. It is protective. God says, "Let Me handle what you were never designed to carry." Bitterness drains energy. Peace restores it.

There is a difference between remembering and reliving. Healing allows you to remember without bleeding. It allows you to tell your story without shaking. It allows you to look back without wanting to hide. This takes time. Peace is not an instant switch. It is a journey. One honest prayer at a time. One boundary at a time. One truth replacing a lie. You may notice that bitterness tries to disguise itself as discernment. Everything feels suspicious. Every leader feels unsafe. Every church feels threatening. While discernment protects, bitterness isolates. Proverbs 4:23 says,

"Guard your heart, for out of it flow the issues of life."

Guarding does not mean closing. It means filtering. You learn to protect your heart without imprisoning it. As peace grows, you stop rehearsing old conversations in your head. You stop needing validation from people who hurt you. You stop proving your innocence. You rest. Peace does not erase memory. It changes how memory affects you. Isaiah 26:3 says,

"You will keep him in perfect peace, whose mind is stayed on You, because he trusts in You."

Perfect peace is not fragile. It is anchored. The Hebrew word for peace, *shalom*, means wholeness, completeness, nothing missing, nothing broken. God's peace is not just calm feelings. It is inner order restored. As bitterness loosens its grip, you begin to breathe again. Literally. Your body relaxes. Your sleep improves. Your prayers feel safer. You stop bracing for impact. You realize that peace is not dependent on people changing. It is dependent on God healing you. This does not mean you stop caring. It means you stop carrying.

Jesus did not harden His heart after betrayal. He entrusted Himself to the Father. *"When He was reviled, He did not revile in return"* (1 Peter 2:23). That was not weakness. That was strength rooted in identity. You are allowed to grieve what you lost. You are allowed to feel sadness over what should have been. Grief clears space for peace. And peace does not make you passive. It makes you free. Free to love again. Free to trust wisely. Free to worship without fear.

The journey from bitterness to peace is sacred work. God walks it with you patiently. He does not rush the process. He honors your pace. You will not always feel strong. But you will feel safe. And one day, you will look back and realize that what once controlled you no longer has power over your heart. That is peace.

Permission to Heal, Recover, And Breathe Again

One of the quiet lies many wounded believers carry is this: *if you are truly healed, you must return to the place that hurt you.* That lie has kept countless people trapped in cycles of pain, confusion, and spiritual exhaustion. Healing does not require reenlistment into harm. God never demanded that broken bones be tested before they were strengthened. He never asked burnt skin to return to fire to prove recovery. In the same way, spiritual healing does not demand that you go back to unsafe environments to validate your faith.

Jesus did not stay where He was rejected. He moved. He withdrew. He rested. He chose timing wisely. And He never apologized for it. Mark 6:31 says,

"Come away by yourselves to a deserted place and rest a while."

This invitation came after ministry, after crowds, after pressure. Jesus understood limits. He honored them. You are allowed to honor yours.

Many believers feel rushed to heal. Pressured to "move on". Urged to "let it go" before wounds have even closed. But God does not rush healing. He leads it. Psalm 147:3 says, *"He heals the brokenhearted and binds up their wounds."* Binding wounds takes time. It is careful, it is intentional, and it requires gentleness. You are not weak because you need time, you are wise. Recovery is not linear. Some days you feel strong. Other days you feel raw. That does not mean you are failing. It means you are human. God does not measure your healing by speed. He measures it by truth. Breathing again is part of healing. Many wounded believers have been holding their breath emotionally for years. Always careful. Always cautious. Always bracing. Healing invites you to exhale. That exhale is permission. Permission to slow down, to say no and to choose peace and calm over noise and chaos.

Jesus said, *"The Sabbath was made for man, not man for the Sabbath"* (Mark 2:27). Rest is not rebellion. It is design. Recovery often begins with boundaries. Boundaries are not walls built from fear. They are doors built from wisdom. Jesus had boundaries. He did not heal everyone in Israel. He did not explain Himself to everyone. He did not submit to every demand. And yet, He was perfectly loving. Boundaries protect what is being rebuilt.

You may need boundaries around conversations. Around church involvement. Around leadership access. Around emotional labor. These boundaries are not signs of bitterness. They are signs of discernment. Proverbs 25:28 says, *"A man without self-control is like a city broken into and left without walls."* Boundaries restore walls. Not to imprison you, but to protect you. Recovery also means redefining spirituality. For some, church attendance became the sole measure of faithfulness. Service replaced intimacy. Activity replaced rest. Healing invites a reset.

Your worth is not tied to attendance. Your faith is not measured by exhaustion. Your devotion is not proven by pain. God meets you in stillness as much as in service. Isaiah 30:15 says,

"In returning and rest you shall be saved; in quietness and confidence shall be your strength."

Strength grows in quiet places. You are allowed to heal without explaining yourself to everyone. You are allowed to step back without guilt. You are allowed to recover privately. Jesus often healed people and told them not to announce it immediately. Healing does not need an audience.

Breathing again also means releasing spiritual performance. Prayer becomes honest again, worship becomes safe again, and silence becomes peaceful instead of threatening. You stop forcing yourself to feel things you do not feel. You start trusting that God meets you where you are. Healing is not pretending. It is aligning with truth. There may be moments when old fears surface. When memories return. When trust feels fragile. This does not mean healing has failed. It means layers are being uncovered. God heals in layers because we can only carry truth in stages. In the book of Psalm 34:18, it says,

"The Lord is near to the brokenhearted and saves those who are crushed in spirit."

Nearness is God's strategy. He does not shout from afar. He stays close. Recovery is not isolation. It is intentional solitude. It is choosing safe people. It is choosing nourishment over noise. You may need new rhythms. New spaces. New voices. This is not disloyalty, it is wisdom.

Permission to heal also includes permission to feel joy again. Some wounded believers feel guilty when they start feeling lighter. As if peace betrays pain. But joy does not erase what you went through. It honors what you survived. Ecclesiastes 3 says there is a time for everything. Including laughter. Breathing again means trusting that your future is not ruined by your past. God does not waste wounds. He redeems them. But redemption does not mean reuse of trauma. It means transformation of identity.

You are not behind. You are not broken beyond repair. You are not disappointing God. You are healing. And healing often looks quiet. Unspectacular. Slow. Gentle. As you recover, you will notice your nervous system calming. Your reactions are softening. Your spirit resting. You will feel less urgency to prove anything.

You will breathe. And in that breath, you will realize something powerful, which is that in spite of the abuse from your church family, God never left you; he does not rush you nor demand you return to pain. He is waiting patiently for you and will heal and teach you how to love your church and the body of Christ again.

Chapter Twelve:

When You Feel Far From God Because Of Church Hurt

Recovering Trust in God after Misplaced Trust in Leaders

There is a particular kind of pain that comes when the people who introduced you to God are the same people who made you feel unsafe with Him. It leaves you confused and torn. You still believe in God, but something inside you flinches when His name is mentioned. Prayer feels awkward. Worship feels distant. Church language feels heavy. I want to tell you that you are not crazy for feeling this way.

Many believers did not walk away from God because they stopped loving Him. They stepped back because trusting Him began to feel risky after trusting people who represented Him and getting hurt. This is where healing must begin. With honesty. The book of Psalm 146:3 says,

"Do not put your trust in princes, in human beings, who cannot save."

That verse is not cynical. It is merciful. God warned us early that humans have limits. Even anointed ones. Even gifted ones. Even well-meaning ones. But when you first came into faith, you may not have known this. You trusted leaders deeply. You believed their words carried God's heart. You followed without filters. That is not foolishness. That is hunger. The problem was not your trust. It was where it was placed. Human failure has a way of casting shadows over God's image. When leaders manipulate, abuse authority, shame, control, or abandon, the mind quietly connects the dots. If this is what God allows… maybe this is who God is.

That thought is rarely spoken aloud. But it sits in the heart. Jesus addressed this clearly. In Matthew 23:3, speaking of religious leaders, He said, *"Do not do according to their works; for they say and do not do."* He separated God's truth from human behavior. He refused to let flawed vessels redefine the Father. You must do the same.

Trust breaks when expectations are crushed. And often, what was broken was not trust in God, but trust in people who were standing too close to His place in your heart. Some leaders were trusted like saviors. Some voices were obeyed without discernment. Some systems demanded loyalty that belonged only to God. When those systems failed, it felt like God failed. But God never asked to be replaced by a leader. Jeremiah 17:5 says,

"Cursed is the one who trusts in man, who draws strength from mere flesh and whose heart turns away from the Lord."

That verse is not a curse aimed at you. It is a warning meant to protect you. God does not want your faith built on fragile foundations.

Rebuilding trust starts with reassigning responsibility. God is responsible for who He is. People are responsible for who they choose to be. Human failure does not equal divine absence. Psalm 118:8 says,

"It is better to trust in the Lord than to put confidence in man."

Better does not mean easier. It means safer. Trusting God again may feel scary because you trusted sincerely before and got hurt. Your heart learnt caution. That is normal human behavior. Pain teaches the body to protect itself. But God is not offended by your hesitation. He is patient with it. Jesus never forced trust. He invited it. After the resurrection, Thomas doubted. Jesus did not shame him. He said, *"Reach your finger here"* (John 20:27). God meets wounded trust with gentleness, not pressure. Rebuilding confidence in God's goodness takes separating experiences from truth. Experiences are real, but they are not final authorities. The goodness of God is not defined by how leaders treated you. It is defined by who God has always been. Exodus 34:6 reveals God describing Himself:

"The Lord, the Lord God, merciful and gracious, longsuffering, and abounding in goodness and truth."

This description came long before church systems existed. Before denominations. Before pulpits. God's nature predates religion.

One reason trust collapses is because leaders were unconsciously elevated into God's role. Their approval felt like God's approval. Their rejection felt like God's rejection. Their silence felt like heaven's silence. That is too much weight for any human to carry. The book of Psalm 27:10 says, *"When my father and my mother forsake me, then the Lord will take me up."* If God can separate Himself from even parental failure, He can separate Himself from spiritual authority failure too.

You are allowed to grieve misplaced trust without abandoning faith. You are allowed to admit disappointment without being accused of rebellion. Healing begins when you stop defending God for what He did not do. God did not manipulate you. God did not silence you. God did not exploit your loyalty. People did. God is not fragile. He can handle the truth. When trust is misplaced, God gently redirects it, not punishes it. He invites you to know Him personally, beyond intermediaries. Jeremiah 9:23–24 says not to boast in wisdom, strength, or riches, *"but let him who boasts boast in this, that he understands and knows Me."* God wants to be known directly. Rebuilding trust also means adjusting expectations. God is consistent. People are not. God is faithful. People are learning.

You do not rebuild trust by forcing closeness. You rebuild it by watching character over time. God invites you to observe Him. Again, Psalm 34:8 says, *"Taste and see that the Lord is good."* Taste implies experience, not theory. 'See' implies awareness, not blindness. Trust grows when you notice how God treats you in private. When He comforts you without condemning you. When He speaks without pressure. He stays when others leave.

Little by little, the fog lifts. God was never the source of your pain. He was present while it happened, grieving with you, waiting for the moment you would look at Him again without fear. You may not trust easily again. That's okay. God is not in a hurry. He is steady. He is kind. And He is still worthy of your heart.

Separating God's Character from Man's Failure

One of the most painful realizations after church hurt is recognizing that God is not the same as those who represent Him.

When leaders fail, we often conflate human flaws with divine character. We think, *"If they betrayed me, then God must have abandoned me too."* But that is a lie the enemy uses to keep your heart in chains. You must unlearn this intentionally. The Bible is clear: God's character is immutable. Malachi 3:6 says, *"For I am the Lord; I do not change."* This is not abstract theology. It is a lifeline for every believer who has been wounded by people who claimed God's authority. God's love, mercy, and justice are consistent, even when human leadership is inconsistent.

Consider how many times God worked through flawed vessels: Moses, David, and Peter, but the imperfections of these servants did not compromise God's heart. Moses struggled with anger (Numbers 20:10), David sinned grievously (2 Samuel 11), and Peter denied Jesus (Luke 22:61). And yet, God's mission prevailed, His plans advanced, and His character remained faithful. What lessons can you take from this? One: human failure does not nullify God's truth. Two: your hurt does not redefine who God is. And three: God's presence is not contingent on human perfection.

Separating God from man begins with redefining your expectations. People will disappoint; God never will. Jeremiah 17:7–8 paints a beautiful picture:

"Blessed is the man who trusts in the Lord, whose confidence is in Him. He will be like a tree planted by the water... it will not fear when heat comes; its leaves will be green, and it will not be anxious in the year of drought."

God is your secure well, even when those around you dry up.

Now, let's address what often trips up wounded believers: associating God's discipline with human manipulation. Many church systems use guilt, shame, or spiritual pressure disguised as holiness. These methods warp perception. They make God seem harsh, distant, or punishing. But Hebrews 12:6 reminds us,

"For the Lord disciplines the one he loves, and chastises every son whom he receives."

Notice the distinction: God's correction is loving and purposeful, not manipulative or fear-driven. Human abuse, however, is arbitrary and self-serving and leaves trauma in its wake. That difference matters.

It is also essential to understand God's heart toward the marginalized and wounded. Psalm 34:18 says, *"The Lord is near to the brokenhearted and saves the crushed in spirit."* Here is a God who does not abandon you to human cruelty but draws close to your pain. You can experience His nearness without needing human approval. You can pray without fearing judgment. You can worship without anxiety. God's character is a refuge, not a source of fear.

Part of separating God from man involves unpacking the emotional baggage tied to church trauma. Ask yourself: Are your feelings of distance based on God's actions or someone else's failures? Often, it is the latter. Human sins are tangible, visible, and hurtful. God's ways are perfect, loving, and consistent. Isaiah 55:8–9 reminds us,

"For my thoughts are not your thoughts, neither are your ways my ways," declares the Lord. For as the heavens are higher than the earth, so are my ways higher than your ways and my thoughts than your thoughts."

God's ways surpass human reasoning. When a church system hurts you, it does not reflect His intentions; it reflects human limitation.

Another practical step is to actively meditate on God's attributes. Write down scriptures that define His goodness, faithfulness, and love. Proverbs 3:5–6 encourages,

"Trust in the Lord with all your heart and lean not on your own understanding; in all your ways acknowledge Him, and He will make your paths straight."

When you consciously acknowledge God's character, you create mental and spiritual separation between Him and human failure. Your heart begins to recalibrate, and trust slowly restores.

Forgiveness toward those who wounded you is not optional; it is freeing. Forgiveness is not forgetting, excusing, or condoning the wrong done. It is releasing the grip that bitterness has on your heart. Ephesians 4:31–32 instructs,

"Let all bitterness and wrath and anger and clamor and slander be put away from you, along with all malice. Be kind to one another, tenderhearted, forgiving one another, as God in Christ forgave you."

As you forgive, you reclaim your peace. You also protect the integrity of God's image in your mind from being tangled with human imperfection.

You must also redefine authority in your own life. Romans 8:38–39 declares that nothing can separate you from the love of God. Human authority may fail. Societal authority may falter. Spiritual authority may misuse its power. Yet God remains sovereign, loving, and constant. Internalizing this truth keeps your faith intact, even in the face of repeated disappointment.

Finally, allow God to restore intimacy on your terms. Do not rush back into environments that mimic past wounds. Instead, cultivate private devotion, personal prayer, and Scripture meditation. Experience His presence independently of others. Let the Spirit guide you into a trust that is informed by experience but not marred by betrayal. Psalm 91:1–2 says,

"He who dwells in the shelter of the Most High will abide in the shadow of the Almighty. I will say to the Lord, 'My refuge and my fortress, my God, in whom I trust.'"

This is not theory. It is a promise for your present reality.

Separating God's character from man's failure is a daily choice. Each time memories of past hurt rise, remind yourself: God did not abandon you. God is not manipulative. God is not cruel, Human failure cannot redefine Him. The church may have failed, the system may have failed, and leaders may have failed, but God is steady. He is trustworthy. He is healing. And His love never wavers.

You are invited to step fully into this truth today: God is not your pain. God is not your disappointment. God is your unfailing refuge.

And He will meet you right where you are, rebuilding your faith, renewing your trust, and restoring the wonder of His presence in your heart. This is the ultimate freedom: experiencing God unfiltered by human imperfection. The God who loves you endlessly, heals you quietly, and restores your spirit wholly. That is your inheritance. Claim it and be changed by it.

Chapter Thirteen:

The Healing Father: Knowing God Anew

Encountering the God Who Restores Your Spiritual Confidence

One of the most heartbreaking consequences of spiritual abuse is the erosion of trust, not just in people, but in God Himself. The very One we're supposed to run to for refuge feels distant, unapproachable, or even untrustworthy. It is as if the hurt that we've suffered at the hands of spiritual leaders has somehow clouded our perception of the Father's heart. But God, in His relentless love, desires to restore your spiritual confidence. He is the healer of broken hearts, and He specializes in rebuilding shattered trust.

When you've been wounded in a place where you were supposed to feel safe, like the church, it is easy to confuse the wounds of people with the character of God. Hurt often distorts our view of God, making it hard to believe that He is truly for us. However, God does not rush the healing process; He does not force Himself into our pain. He is a gentle Father, one who whispers His love when we're most vulnerable. Just like a loving parent comforts a crying child, God patiently draws near to us, inviting us into a space where healing can begin.

There is a scripture that paints a beautiful picture of this: *"The Lord is near to the brokenhearted and saves those who are crushed in spirit"* (Psalm 34:18, NIV). This is not a cold, impersonal promise; this is the intimate reassurance that God's heart beats for you, especially when your heart is hurting. God does not turn away when you are broken; He draws near. He is not in a hurry, but He is always willing to sit with you in your pain, offering His tender comfort.

Consider the story of Elijah, after his encounter with the prophets of Baal, when he fled into the wilderness, fearful and broken. He ran from the very calling that had once stirred his heart. Yet God, in His mercy, did not chastise him for his fears. Instead, He provided food, rest, and a gentle whisper in the midst of the storm (1 Kings 19:11-12). God knows the depth of your pain, and He responds not with condemnation but with care and comfort. He meets you where you are, not where you should be. He rebuilds your spiritual confidence piece by piece, slowly restoring what was lost, giving you the courage to trust again.

The restoration of spiritual confidence isn't just about fixing trust in God; it is about reclaiming your identity as a beloved child of God. Abusive environments often twist your understanding of who you are. You might feel like you've lost your place in God's kingdom, as if your wounds somehow disqualify you from His love. But that's a lie. You were never meant to be defined by the wounds of others; you are defined by the blood of Christ.

In those moments of healing, God does not just restore your trust in Him; He reminds you of who you are in Him. The apostle Paul beautifully writes, *"For you are all sons of God through faith in Christ Jesus"* (Galatians 3:26, NKJV). You are not a victim of your past. You are not defined by the hurts that have shaped your journey.

You are a child of God. This is your true identity, and God's desire is to bring you into a deep realization of that.

When Jesus encountered Peter after his denial, He did not condemn him for his failures. Instead, He reinstated him, asking, *"Do you love me?"* (John 21:15-17). Each time Peter affirmed his love, Jesus gave him a commission: *"Feed my sheep."* This wasn't just a restoration of Peter's position; it was a reaffirmation of his identity. He wasn't just a disciple anymore; he was the one entrusted to lead others. God does not just heal; He redeems. He does not just fix the broken parts of us; He calls us back to purpose.

You may have felt forgotten or abandoned, but God is reminding you today that you belong. His invitation to you is to sit at His table, to receive His love, and to stand in the fullness of your identity as His child. No mistake, no hurt, no failure can strip you of the love and acceptance He has for you.

God is not just the restorer of your confidence; He is also the guide who leads you forward. In the midst of confusion, when all you want to do is run and hide, God is there, gently guiding you to a place of peace. His direction is sure, steady, and unfailing. He does not leave you in the wilderness of uncertainty but beckons you forward, showing you the way.

The psalmist declares, *"Your word is a lamp to my feet and a light to my path"* (Psalm 119:105, NIV). God's Word is more than a set of instructions; it is a constant reminder of His presence, guiding you, leading you, and lighting your way even in the darkest moments. The beauty of receiving divine reassurance and direction is that it often comes in small, quiet moments. It is the whisper of His peace in your heart. It is the encouragement from a trusted friend. It is the still, small voice that speaks truth to your spirit when the lies of the enemy try to drown you in confusion.

There will be times when the road ahead seems unclear, when you do not know what your next step should be. But God promises that He will not leave you without guidance.

"For the Lord will be your confidence and will keep your foot from being caught" (Proverbs 3:26, NKJV).

You do not have to have all the answers right now. What you need is to trust that He has already paved the way for you, even if you cannot see it yet. Trust in His perfect timing and His perfect wisdom.

Just like the Israelites wandering in the desert, you might feel like you are in a season of uncertainty. But remember, even in the desert, God provided; He provided manna, water, and His presence in the form of a cloud by day and a fire by night (Exodus 13:21-22). Even in your wilderness, God is leading you with purpose, and He will not abandon you. Trust that He has a plan for your future, a plan that is full of hope and restoration. He is gently guiding you out of the wilderness of spiritual confusion into the promised land of peace and clarity.

Hearing God's Voice Again after Silence and Confusion

There is a special kind of ache that comes when you no longer hear God the way you once did. You pray, but the words feel like they hit the ceiling and fall back down. You read Scripture, but it feels flat, like a familiar song played with no sound. You remember a time when God's voice felt close, clear, and alive, and now there is quiet. Not peaceful quiet but confusing quiet. If you have been there, this is for you.

Silence after hurt does not mean God stopped speaking. It often means your soul learnt to protect itself. When you were wounded in a sacred space, your heart did what hearts do—it closed a window to survive the storm. You did not lose spiritual sensitivity because you were rebellious or lazy. You lost it because pain is loud, and fear crowds the room.

Scripture shows this pattern again and again. Elijah, fresh from victory, ran into the wilderness exhausted and afraid. When God came near, He was not in the wind, the earthquake, or the fire. He was in the still small voice (1 Kings 19:12). The Hebrew phrase there points to a gentle whisper, not a shout. God was not competing with Elijah's chaos. He waited for it to settle.

Hurt often blocks spiritual sensitivity because pain demands attention. When your heart is busy bracing itself, it cannot easily discern whispers. Think of it like this: when your house has been broken into, every sound feels like danger. Even friendly footsteps make you tense. In the same way, after betrayal or spiritual harm, your inner world becomes alert, guarded, and tired. You are listening for threat, not for tenderness.

This is why God does not rush you back into hearing. He restores safety first.

Jesus said, "My sheep hear My voice, and I know them, and they follow Me" (John 10:27). Hearing God's voice is tied to relationship, not performance. The Greek word for "hear" here is *akouō*, which means to listen with understanding and attention. It is not just sound entering the ear. It is connection. When trust is shaken, *akouō* becomes difficult—not impossible, just delayed. God understands this. He does not punish silence with more silence. He responds with patience.

One of the first ways God reopens the channels of communication is by changing the pressure around you. He removes the noise that once defined spirituality for you. Less striving. Less performing. Less trying to impress heaven. You may notice that God begins to speak through simple things again. A verse that suddenly breathes, a moment of peace that makes no sense, a quiet nudge instead of a command.

This is not God becoming distant, this is God becoming gentle. Psalm 46:10 says, *"Be still, and know that I am God."* The phrase "be still" comes from the Hebrew *raphah*, which means to let go, to loosen your grip, and to stop striving. Knowing God again begins with unclenching. You cannot hear clearly with a fist clenched around your heart.

You may also notice that God's voice now carries a different tone than before. Less fear. More assurance. Less urgency. More clarity. God does not shout to control you. He speaks to lead you. If what you are hearing is harsh, condemning, or panic-driven, pause. That is not His voice. Romans 8:15 reminds you that you did not receive the spirit of bondage again to fear, but the Spirit of adoption, by whom you cry, "Abba, Father." God's voice sounds like belonging.

Discerning God's voice from emotional noise takes practice, but it is simpler than you may think. Emotional noise is reactive. It rushes. It pressures. It accuses. God's voice may correct, but it never shames. It may guide, but it never manipulates. James 3:17 says wisdom from above is first pure, then peaceable, gentle, willing to yield, full of mercy and good fruit. If the voice you are hearing produces peace even when it challenges you, stay with it.

Another sign that God is reopening communication is that He begins to ask questions instead of giving orders. "Where are you?" "What are you afraid of?" "Do you love Me?" God asked Adam questions. He asked Elijah questions. Jesus asked Peter questions. Questions invite healing. Orders enforce control. God is not trying to dominate your will. He is restoring your trust.

You may also find that God speaks more through Scripture now than through impressions alone. This is intentional. Scripture becomes a safe anchor when your emotions feel unreliable. As you read, let the Word read you. Do not rush, sit with a line and let it land. Hebrews 4:12 reminds you that the Word of God is living and active. It knows how to reach places sermons never touched.

Be patient with yourself. Hearing God again is not about volume. It is about familiarity. Like recognizing a loved one's voice in a crowd, it comes with time spent together. Start small. Short prayers. Honest words. Silence without guilt. God is not grading you.

Here is a quiet truth you need to hear clearly: God never stopped speaking your name. You just needed healing ears, and they are healing. You will hear Him again. Not as a tyrant. Not as a threat. But as a Father who knows how to find His child even in the dark.

Chapter Fourteen:

Rebuilding A Healthy Spiritual Life

Steps To Reconnect With Scripture, Prayer and Fellowship Safely

For many who have experienced spiritual hurt or abuse, the thought of returning to spiritual practices can feel overwhelming. Scripture, prayer, and fellowship, those once familiar avenues of connection with God, might now seem distant or even triggering. The truth is, healing requires a careful, gradual reconnection with these practices, not out of obligation, but out of a desire to rediscover God in a safe, restorative way. This chapter will explore how you can begin to return to these spiritual disciplines without pressure, embracing a healthy, sustainable approach to each.

Returning to spiritual practices after a time of emotional and spiritual pain is like mending a broken bone; it takes time, gentleness, and intentional care. You do not rush the healing process, and you do not push yourself to do more than you are ready for. God's invitation is never about demanding performance; it is about drawing near in love. You may feel pressure from others, or even from yourself, but it is important to remember that God meets you where you are, and He is patient with your process.

When it comes to reconnecting with Scripture, start slow. The Bible is not a book to be consumed quickly but a living text meant to speak to your heart. Begin with short passages or verses that speak to healing, love, and restoration. Psalms, for instance, is full of raw emotion and genuine connection with God in the midst of hardship. Let these words wash over you. *"The Lord is close to the brokenhearted and saves those who are crushed in spirit"* (Psalm 34:18, NIV). This verse reminds us that God does not shy away from our pain. Instead, He draws near to heal it.

Do not feel pressured to dive into extensive Bible study or memorization. Just sit with a verse or a passage, and let it be enough. The Holy Spirit will guide you through those moments of quiet reflection, allowing the Word to penetrate your heart in its own time. You can even keep a journal to write down any thoughts or feelings that come to you as you read. This can be a powerful way to record your journey, without the pressure of performance. God does not need perfection; He desires presence.

In prayer, start by being honest with God about where you are. You do not need to have eloquent words. Just speak to Him as you would to a friend. If the thought of praying feels daunting, begin with one simple phrase: "Lord, help me." And then allow silence. Silence is not the absence of prayer but an invitation to hear. God does not need our constant talking; He wants our openness. As you practice this, you may find that prayer begins to feel more natural again.

For fellowship, the key is to find a community that is safe, understanding, and willing to meet you where you are. If you are still hesitant about returning to a church environment, do not rush into it. Maybe start with smaller, intimate gatherings, Bible studies, prayer groups, or even a one-on-one connection with a trusted friend. It is okay to take your time. God's Church should be a place of healing, not pressure. Fellowship is about mutual encouragement, not about fitting into a mold. When you find a group that fosters acceptance and love, your heart will be more open to growth.

Many people who've suffered spiritual abuse have a complex relationship with God's Word. What was once a source of comfort may now feel like a battleground. When Scripture was used to control or manipulate, it is hard to see it as the life-giving truth it is meant to be. Yet, God's Word remains the most powerful tool for healing and restoration; it is living and active, able to cut through the darkness and bring light.

Start by redefining your relationship with the Bible. It is not a weapon to hurt or shame you; it is the voice of a loving Father who desires to restore your soul.

"For the word of God is alive and active. Sharper than any double-edged sword..."

(Hebrews 4:12, NIV).

Let these words remind you that God's Word is powerful, not to condemn, but to heal and set free. When you feel triggered by certain passages, do not force yourself to engage with them right away. Acknowledge your feelings and give yourself permission to step away. God understands your pain and is patient with your journey. Instead of diving immediately into the difficult parts of Scripture, focus on verses that speak of God's love, His grace, and His healing power. Let those truths sink deeply into your heart. Psalms, Matthew, and the letters of Paul offer beautiful expressions of God's mercy, peace, and gentleness. For example,

"Come to me, all you who are weary and burdened, and I will give you rest"

(Matthew 11:28, NIV).

This is an invitation, not a command. It is a promise that when you are weary from life's burdens, God will give you rest, not condemnation, not pressure, but comfort.

Another great approach is to meditate on God's character, rather than focusing on the pressure to understand every verse or chapter right away. Think of the Bible as a mirror that reflects God's heart. When you read it, you are invited to see Him more clearly, not to measure your worth. God's Word reveals His heart for you: kind, merciful, patient, and always ready to restore.

If the idea of reading the Bible still feels heavy, try listening to Scripture instead of reading it. There are many apps and podcasts that offer Scripture readings, and sometimes hearing the Word can be less triggering than reading it on your own. Let God speak through others' voices, allowing the healing Word to enter your heart without any fear of judgment or condemnation.

Fellowship is a vital part of the healing process, but re-engaging with community after being hurt is one of the hardest steps. Many believers are afraid that going back to a church community will only lead to more pain. The key is to take it slow and find a community that prioritizes love, acceptance, and understanding over performance or perfection. Healing happens in safe, grace-filled spaces where people can walk alongside each other without judgment.

Re-engaging in community does not mean you have to jump right back into a large church setting. Start small. Reach out to one or two people who have shown themselves to be supportive and understanding. Spend time with those who have your best interest at heart. Ask God to lead you to a fellowship that nurtures your soul, rather than places unrealistic demands on you.

It is also important to set boundaries when engaging with fellowship. If you feel like a certain group or church isn't honoring your healing process, it is okay to step back and seek out a healthier environment.

"Do not be yoked together with unbelievers. For what do righteousness and wickedness have in common?" (2 Corinthians 6:14, NIV).

This verse does not just apply to relationships with unbelievers; it is also about making sure you are in fellowship with those who honor your spiritual well-being. Be discerning. Guard your heart.

It is also okay to take breaks. It is not failure; it is wisdom. As you re-engage with the community, pace yourself. If you need time alone to process or to rest, take it without guilt. God does not require you to jump back into fellowship the moment you feel the slightest bit better. He knows your heart and will guide you into community at the right time.

Creating Boundaries That Protect Your Peace and Purpose

One of the most essential lessons in healing from church abuse is learning the importance of boundaries, emotional and spiritual boundaries. These are not walls meant to isolate or shut others out, but protective measures to preserve your peace, identity, and spiritual health. Without boundaries, we are vulnerable to being overwhelmed by the emotions, opinions, and manipulations of others. When we've experienced hurt, especially spiritual abuse, creating healthy boundaries is an act of self-care and self-preservation.

Boundaries are biblical. In fact, Jesus Himself established boundaries. He knew when to retreat, when to rest, and when to engage. There is a story in Mark 1:35-38 that perfectly demonstrates this:

"Very early in the morning, while it was still dark, Jesus got up, left the house and went off to a solitary place, where he prayed. Simon and his companions went to look for him, and when they found him, they exclaimed, 'Everyone is looking for you!' Jesus replied, 'Let us go somewhere else, to the nearby villages, so I can preach there also. That is why I have come.'"

(Mark 1:35-38, NIV).

Jesus understood that His purpose could only be fulfilled if He remained grounded and connected to the Father. He did not allow the crowd's demands to dictate His actions.

Similarly, we must learn to set boundaries in our own lives to ensure that we're living out our purpose, not being driven by the needs and pressures of others. Boundaries give us the freedom to say no when necessary, to protect our emotional space, and to ensure that we are engaging in ways that honor our well-being and our calling. Without boundaries, we end up living in reaction to everything around us, constantly at the mercy of others' demands, requests, and criticisms.

Emotional boundaries help us regulate what we allow ourselves to feel and experience, while spiritual boundaries protect our connection to God. We do not have to allow the hurtful words, unrealistic expectations, or emotional manipulation of others to control our peace. In Matthew 7:6, Jesus said,

"Do not give dogs what is sacred; do not throw your pearls to pigs. If you do, they may trample them under their feet and turn and tear you to pieces."

This verse speaks to the need for discernment in where we invest our time, energy, and emotions. Not everyone deserves access to your heart, and not every relationship needs to be nurtured. Boundaries allow you to discern wisely and protect your emotional health.

Without boundaries, we find ourselves caught in cycles, cycles of abuse, manipulation, or neglect. Spiritual abuse thrives where boundaries are either ignored or nonexistent. A leader who refuses to respect your personal space, time, or decisions is creating an environment where abuse can flourish. Similarly, when we do not have healthy emotional boundaries, we may unknowingly allow people to violate our trust repeatedly.

Boundaries are like guards protecting your spiritual and emotional well-being while in the church. They help you determine where others end and where you begin. They allow you to decide what behaviors you will tolerate and what you will not. In the absence of boundaries, we may tolerate toxic behavior for fear of conflict, rejection, or guilt. However, the result is that we end up in an endless loop of being hurt, manipulated, or exploited.

By setting clear boundaries, you can break free from these cycles. Boundaries allow you to walk away from situations that harm you and protect your heart from being re-wounded. In Matthew 18:15-17, Jesus outlines a process for confronting sin in the church, an indication that we are not meant to stay silent or passive when it comes to our well-being.

"If your brother or sister sins, go and point out their fault, just between the two of you. If they listen to you, you have won them over. But if they will not listen, take one or two others along, so that 'every matter may be established by the testimony of two or three witnesses.'"

(Matthew 18:15-16, NIV).

This passage shows that confronting harmful behavior and setting boundaries is a scriptural mandate. We are not to allow cycles of abuse to continue unchecked. Setting boundaries isn't about causing division or strife; it is about protecting our spiritual integrity and ensuring that we engage with others in a healthy, respectful manner. When we make it clear that certain behaviors are unacceptable, we prevent further violations and set the stage for healthier relationships moving forward.

Boundaries also help us guard against being manipulated by false teachings or pressure from toxic church environments. If you are coming out of an abusive church situation, it is important to protect your heart from the emotional coercion that often accompanies such spaces. When the demand for "submission" turns into domination, or when guilt is used as a tactic for control, boundaries protect you from falling back into those cycles. In 1 Corinthians 15:33, Paul writes,

"*Do not be misled: 'Bad Company corrupts good character.'*"

Boundaries help us recognize when we are being influenced by unhealthy company or environments. Setting boundaries allows us to maintain our integrity, protecting us from being pulled back into harmful dynamics. Boundaries are not just about protecting yourself from others; they are also about guarding your God-given purpose. Your purpose is sacred, and you must take steps to protect it emotionally, spiritually, and practically. Without clear boundaries, it is easy to lose sight of your calling, allowing the demands of others, the opinions of well-meaning but misguided people, or the constant pressure of external expectations to derail your path.

When you set boundaries, you set a clear intention for how you will live in alignment with your purpose. Boundaries help you priorities your calling over distractions and interruptions. If you have been in an environment that has discouraged or exploited your gifts, it is essential to take time to rediscover your purpose in God's eyes. Spend time with God, prayerfully seeking clarity on what He has called you to do, and then guard that calling fiercely. In the book of Proverbs 4:23, the word of God says,

"Above all else, guard your heart, for everything you do flows from it."

This is a powerful reminder that your heart, your purpose, your vision, and your spiritual health must be guarded. Guarding your purpose involves setting boundaries that keep you focused on what matters most. It is about saying no to things that pull you away from your calling, even if they seem good or noble. Sometimes, in order to protect your purpose, you must be willing to say no to good things in order to preserve the best things that God has called you to.

Guarding your purpose also means recognizing when you are getting off track. Have you ever found yourself agreeing to do something, only to realize later that it is pulling you away from your true calling? Boundaries protect you from that. They allow you to reassess your commitments and evaluate whether they align with your purpose. As you grow in clarity about your purpose, you'll become better equipped to set limits that allow you to focus on what's truly important.

Ultimately, boundaries help you live with wisdom. They allow you to say yes to things that are aligned with your purpose and no to things that aren't. In Matthew 6:33, Jesus says,

"But seek first His kingdom and His righteousness, and all these things will be given to you as well."

Seeking God's kingdom first means that you priorities your purpose; everything else flows from that decision.

Chapter Fifteen:

Returning To Community Without Losing Yourself

How to Discern Safe Churches and Safe Leaders

After experiencing church hurt or spiritual abuse, returning to community can feel like walking into the unknown. Trust has been broken, and there is a deep sense of vulnerability. The thought of re-engaging with a church community may fill you with both hope and dread. How do you know if a church is truly safe? How do you discern whether a leader is healthy or harmful? These questions are crucial because the wrong environment can perpetuate your wounds, while the right one can be a place of healing and growth.

The first step in discerning a safe church is understanding what a healthy church culture looks like. The Bible gives us clear markers of what to look for. Healthy leadership and church culture will reflect humility, servant leadership, and a genuine commitment to the well-being of its members. Jesus exemplified the perfect leader when He washed His disciples' feet (John 13:14-15), showing that true leadership is not about power but service. Healthy leaders do not demand worship or submission; they lead by example and encourage others to grow in their relationship with Christ.

In a safe church, leadership is not about control or dominance but about nurturing spiritual growth and creating an environment where all can thrive. A healthy church fosters a culture of openness and vulnerability, where individuals can express their struggles and find support. There is a genuine emphasis on mutual accountability, grace, and love, qualities that are essential in any healthy community.

Consider Paul's letter to the Ephesians, where he encourages believers to "be completely humble and gentle; be patient, bearing with one another in love" (Ephesians 4:2, NIV). The church leadership should be patient and humble, not forcing people to meet unrealistic expectations, but lovingly guiding them towards spiritual growth. The true role of a leader is to empower others, not control them.

A safe church also creates an environment of transparency. It is a place where you do not feel like you have to hide your struggles or pretend to be someone you are not. Leaders are open about their own struggles, showing that they are real people in need of God's grace, just like everyone else. This fosters an environment of trust, where you can feel safe to be yourself and not live under the pressure of perfection.

On the other hand, there are red flags that indicate a church or leader is unsafe. First, watch for any signs of authoritarian control. A leader who demands unquestioning loyalty, who manipulates people with fear, or who isolates individuals from outside influence is a major red flag. Scripture warns us against such leadership. In 1 Peter 5:3, leaders are exhorted, *"Not lording it over those entrusted to you, but being examples to the flock."* A safe leader does not lord over others; they lead by example, allowing people the space to make their own decisions in freedom.

Another red flag is when a church emphasizes performance over relationship. If you feel like you have to constantly prove your worth, earn your place, or perform in order to belong, that's not a healthy church. The gospel tells us that we are accepted by grace, not by our works (Ephesians 2:8-9). If a church makes you feel that your worth is determined by what you do, it is a sign that something is wrong.

Unhealthy churches also tend to avoid accountability. When leaders do not submit to any form of external oversight or when questions are discouraged, it is a major warning sign. Leaders who cannot be held accountable to others are often the ones who will abuse their power, leading to spiritual manipulation and harm.

Finally, churches that operate in secrecy or have a "do as I say, not as I do" mentality are not safe places. The Apostle Paul, in his letter to the Philippians, urged them to *"join together in following my example"* (Philippians 3:17, NIV). A leader should be able to model what they preach. If a leader's actions do not align with their teachings, that's a clear indication that they may not be leading with integrity.

Spiritual discernment is essential for navigating your way through community after church hurt. It involves listening to God's voice, being sensitive to the Holy Spirit's leading, and using wisdom in your interactions with others. Discernment helps you understand when to engage and when to step back, when to speak and when to remain silent. The good news is that God has given us tools for discernment, and they are available to all believers.

The first tool is prayer. James 1:5 encourages us, *"If any of you lacks wisdom, let him ask of God, who gives to all liberally and without reproach, and it will be given to him."* Prayer is not just about asking God for what we want; it is about asking Him for clarity, for wisdom, and for the ability to see things as they truly are. In times of uncertainty, ask God for wisdom to discern the health of a church and its leaders.

The second tool is Scripture. God's Word is a lamp to our feet, guiding us in the right direction (Psalm 119:105). When you are unsure about a church or a leader, look to the Bible for guidance. If a leader or church is not aligning with the truths of Scripture, then it is a clear sign to step away. God's Word never fails to reveal what is true and good.

Another important tool is community. No one is meant to walk this journey alone. Surround yourself with wise, godly friends who can help you discern what is healthy and what isn't. Proverbs 15:22 tells us,

"Plans fail for lack of counsel, but with many advisers, they succeed."

Having a group of trusted individuals who are spiritually mature can help you navigate tricky situations and make sound decisions.

It is also important that you are patient with the process. Discernment does not happen overnight. It takes time, and sometimes it requires trial and error. Trust that God is leading you to the right place, and give yourself the space to grow in your ability to discern. Be willing to listen to God's voice, and do not rush the process.

Finding A Spiritual Home That Respects Your Humanity And Destiny

Finding a spiritual home after experiencing hurt can feel like both a daunting and liberating process. After all, the Church is meant to be a safe place, a sanctuary where believers are nurtured, supported, and encouraged in their walk with God. Yet, for many who have been wounded by church abuse, the thought of returning to any form of community can stir up anxiety, fear, and hesitation.

So, how do you choose a spiritual home that will honor your journey, meet you where you are, and encourage your healing and growth? It is crucial to remember that your worth and your spiritual journey are not defined by your past experiences but by God's call on your life. A healthy church will recognize that and will welcome you with open arms as you are, without any conditions, expectations, or demands. This is not about you fitting into their mold; it is about finding a community that can meet you where you are and nurture your growth, free from judgment or manipulation.

The first step in choosing a community that honors your journey is knowing your worth. God has created you uniquely, with purpose and destiny. When you step into a church, you should feel valued for who you are, not for what you can do for the church. A healthy community will see you as a person, not a project, and will affirm your dignity. You do not have to prove anything. God already sees you as His beloved.

Look for a church where authenticity is encouraged. This means a church where people can be open about their struggles, their questions, and their doubts. A community that creates space for vulnerability and honesty is one where you can truly heal. When you feel accepted and heard, you'll begin to feel safe enough to grow, knowing that your humanity is not just accepted but embraced.

This church will not demand that you "snap back" to normal or rush your recovery process. It will honors the pace of your journey, understanding that healing from spiritual abuse is not an overnight process. *"Come to me, all you who are weary and burdened, and I will give you rest"* (Matthew 11:28, NIV). A church that honors your journey recognizes that rest is part of healing and that you are allowed to step into community at your own pace.

A key indicator of a healthy church is how it nurtures the identity and calling of its members. When we experience abuse or manipulation in a church environment, it can deeply damage our sense of self. We may feel as though we've lost sight of who we are or what we're called to do. In contrast, a church that values your identity in Christ will help you rediscover and grow in your calling.

A healthy church helps you see yourself the way God sees you. Ephesians 2:10 says,

"For we are God's handiwork, created in Christ Jesus to do good works, which God prepared in advance for us to do."

This verse reminds us that God has uniquely designed each of us for a specific purpose. A church that nurtures identity will affirm that your calling is unique and that your value is not tied to your past mistakes, failures, or hurts. Instead, they will encourage you to grow into the person God has always intended you to be.

One of the ways a church nurtures identity is by speaking truth into your life. In many cases, spiritual abuse leads to distorted views of self-worth, but a healthy church community helps you return to a biblically grounded understanding of who you are. For instance, when God speaks to Moses in Exodus 3:10-12, He does not define Moses by his past failure or self-doubt but calls him to His purpose, saying,

"So now, go. I am sending you to Pharaoh to bring my people, the Israelites, out of Egypt."

The calling wasn't based on Moses' own strength or abilities, but on God's power and plan. Similarly, a healthy church helps you see that your identity is rooted in Christ, and your calling is about fulfilling His purpose for you, not about meeting the expectations of others.

A church that nurtures your identity also gives you the opportunity to serve in ways that align with your gifts and passions. Your calling isn't just about what you can do within the walls of a church; it is about how God has uniquely gifted you to serve the world. Healthy churches empower people to use their gifts, whether in teaching, service, leadership, or creativity, in ways that honors God and bless others. They understand that your calling is part of God's greater plan, and they encourage you to explore it fully.

A church that nurtures calling does not push you into service for the sake of duty but helps you discover the areas where your heart and God's will intersect. They create an environment where you can explore your passions, step into leadership roles when you are ready, and be celebrated for the unique gifts you bring.

Another important aspect of choosing a spiritual home that respects your journey is understanding the importance of your voice, needs, and boundaries. If you've experienced church hurt, you've likely felt that your voice did not matter. You might have been silenced, ignored, or manipulated into staying quiet. A healthy church will encourage you to find your voice and use it, not only in worship but also in the life of the church.

Your voice matters to God, and it should matter in the community you belong to. A healthy church will create space for you to speak your truth, ask questions, and offer feedback. *"Let everything that has breath praise the Lord"* (Psalm 150:6). Praise is not just through song but also through sharing your perspective, your wisdom, and your experiences. If a church values your voice, it will listen. It will respect your thoughts, honors your experiences, and invite you to contribute to the body of Christ.

In addition to your voice, your needs matter. A healthy church does not just take; it also gives. It recognizes that you have emotional, spiritual, and practical needs that deserve attention and care. Just as the early church shared their resources and supported each other (Acts 2:44-45), a healthy church is one where your needs are taken seriously. If you are going through a difficult season, a safe community will step in to help, whether through prayer, emotional support, or practical assistance.

Boundaries are perhaps one of the hardest things to implement after experiencing spiritual abuse. We often feel guilty about setting limits, especially in a church environment where there is pressure to always give, always serve, and always be available. But boundaries are a way to protect your peace and purpose. Just as Jesus set boundaries by withdrawing to pray (Mark 1:35), you too need the freedom to step away when needed, to say no when necessary, and to take care of yourself.

Boundaries help you maintain your spiritual health. They prevent burnout, protect your emotional space, and ensure that you do not give so much that you lose yourself in the process. *"Above all else, guard your heart, for everything you do flows from it"* (Proverbs 4:23, NIV). Guarding your heart includes setting boundaries that allow you to stay grounded in God's purpose for you. A church that respects your boundaries will not manipulate you into serving beyond your capacity. Instead, it will honors your needs, offering support and understanding as you grow and heal. It will help you find balance between service and rest, between community engagement and personal time.

A spiritual home that respects your humanity and destiny is one that honors who you are, values your voice, and protects your peace. It nurtures your identity and calling, allowing you to grow without fear or pressure. As you seek out this kind of community, remember that God has designed you with purpose, and He wants you to flourish in a place where you can fully embrace who He created you to be.

Chapter Sixteen:

When God Sends You Back As A Healer

Turning Your Pain into Ministry without Carrying Poison

Pain has a funny way of shaping us. It either molds us into something stronger, or it can leave us with sharp edges, ready to hurt anyone who gets too close. When you've been wounded, whether spiritually, emotionally, or physically, there is a temptation to let that pain define you. You might start thinking of yourself as a victim, a walking reminder of all the things that went wrong. Or, you might feel as though you are not allowed to heal and move forward. The truth, though, is that God does not waste pain. He uses it to shape you into a vessel of healing for others.

But there is a difference between turning your pain into ministry and carrying around poison. If you are not careful, you may start to minister to others from a place of hurt and bitterness, inadvertently pouring out all the negativity, anger, and unresolved issues onto others. When you try to minister from a broken heart without dealing with your pain, you end up bleeding on those you are supposed to be helping. It is like offering someone a cup of water while your own glass is cracked and leaking all over the place. What can you give if you are not whole yourself?

God does not want to send you out as a healer when you are still carrying the poison of bitterness and unresolved wounds. Healing must happen before ministry. Your story is powerful, but it needs to be processed through God's lens before it can be a source of strength for others. This is a key lesson: healing does not mean forgetting your wounds; it means using them to help others without being controlled by them. In 2 Corinthians 1:3-4, Paul writes,

"Praise be to the God and Father of our Lord Jesus Christ, the Father of compassion and the God of all comfort, who comforts us in all our troubles, so that we can comfort those in any trouble with the comfort we ourselves receive from God."

Your pain is not for nothing. God's comfort to you is meant to overflow into others' lives. But here is the catch: you can only comfort others with the comfort you've received. If you haven't allowed God to fully heal you, then the comfort you offer will be incomplete. Think of it like a tree. The tree can only produce fruit if it has been watered, nourished, and allowed to grow. If the tree hasn't received what it needs, it will produce sour or shriveled fruit. Similarly, if you haven't allowed God to heal you, your ministry will be tainted by your own unresolved pain, and it might end up hurting others rather than helping them. When God sends you back as a healer, He is not asking you to ignore your wounds. He is asking you to let Him heal them first. This might take time, but it is worth it. When He does send you out, you'll be like a well of living water that brings life, not a bitter spring that leaves others thirsty for healing.

Your story is uniquely yours, and it is important to understand that it is not defined by the pain or abuse you've experienced. God wants to help you see your story through His eyes, through a lens of redemption, grace, and hope. If all you see is hurt, it can be hard to believe that anything good can come from it. But God is in the business of turning ashes into beauty (Isaiah 61:3), and He can take the broken pieces of your past and create something beautiful out of them.

One of the first steps in processing your story through God's lens is forgiveness. You may feel that forgiveness is impossible, especially when it comes to those who have caused you pain. But forgiveness is not about excusing someone's behavior or letting them off the hook. It is about releasing the hold that pain has on your heart. It is a way of saying, "I will not let this hurt define me anymore. I choose to let go of this weight so I can move forward and be healed."

Jesus teaches us the importance of forgiveness in Matthew 18:21-22, when He tells Peter that we must forgive *"seventy-seven times"*, not just seven times. Forgiveness is not a one-time event; it is a continual process of releasing the offence and allowing God to heal our hearts. In doing so, we free ourselves from the grip of bitterness and anger.

Once you've begun the process of forgiveness, it is time to look at your story through God's eyes. Instead of viewing your past as a series of unfortunate events or a trail of brokenness, begin to see how God's grace has carried you through each moment. He has never left you, even in your darkest hours. Psalm 34:18 says, *"The Lord is close to the brokenhearted and saves those who are crushed in spirit."* He was there when you felt abandoned, when you thought you could not take another step. He has been weaving your story with threads of grace, mercy, and love, even when you could not see it.

Processing your story through God's lens means acknowledging the pain but also recognizing the redemptive work He has done in you. Your story, as painful as it may have been, is now part of the tapestry of His grace. God can take your mess and turn it into a message, and He can use your wounds to heal others. This is what ministry from a healed heart looks like: It is not pretending the pain never happened; it is acknowledging it, processing it with God, and then using it to bring hope to others.

Showing How To Minister Without Bleeding On Others

When you minister from a place of brokenness without allowing God to heal you first, you end up bleeding on others. It is as though you are offering them something with one hand, while the other hand is still clutching your wounds. The problem is that when you haven't fully healed, your pain starts to dictate how you serve. You may become angry, resentful, or judgmental. You may unintentionally project your unhealed emotions onto the people you are trying to help.

In order to minister without bleeding on others, you need to allow God to do the work in you first. This does not mean you wait until you are perfect; it means you recognize that you are in a process of healing, and you invite God to continue that work while you minister. When Jesus healed people, He did not do it out of His own brokenness; He did it out of His divine nature, which is whole, complete, and perfect. As His followers, we are called to minister from that same place of wholeness, even if we're still in the process of healing.

The key is to minister out of compassion, not out of unhealed pain. Compassion is different from sympathy. Compassion seeks to heal, while sympathy can sometimes just mirror the hurt without offering a path forward. In Matthew 9:36, Jesus looked at the crowds with compassion because He saw them as *"harassed and helpless, like sheep without a shepherd."* He wasn't just feeling sorry for them; he was moved to action. Compassion leads you to care for others and offer them the hope and healing that God has given you. It does not bleed on them. It uplifts and restores.

Before you step into a healing ministry, ask yourself, "Have I allowed God to heal me first? Am I ministering from a place of wholeness, or am I still carrying unhealed wounds?" The goal is to be a vessel of God's love, not a vessel of hurt. When God heals you, your ministry will overflow with His love, not your bitterness.

Ministering To Others Who Have Suffered Church Abuse

One of the most sacred calls of a believer is to minister to those who are suffering, especially those who have been hurt by the very place they once believed would be their refuge: the church. Church abuse is a deep wound, and if you have walked through it yourself, you know the complexities of the pain. It is not just the disappointment of human error; it is the spiritual confusion, the mistrust, and the feeling of being betrayed by people who were meant to represent Christ's love.

As someone who has experienced church hurt and healing, you are now in a unique position to help others. But it is important to approach this responsibility with great care and humility. Ministering to others who are suffering from church abuse is not about offering quick fixes or rushing them through their healing journey. It is about walking alongside them with empathy, listening to their pain, and sharing the healing hope that Christ has given you.

Empathy is key. It is the ability to feel with others, to stand in their shoes, and to understand their emotions without judgment. It is easy to tell someone, "It'll be okay" or "God's got you," but that's not what people who have been hurt need. They do not need to be fixed; they need to be heard, understood, and validated. In Romans 12:15, Paul urges us to *"Rejoice with those who rejoice; mourn with those who mourn."* To truly minister to someone who is hurting, you must enter into their grief. Do not try to rush them through their emotions; give them the space to grieve and process their pain. Show them that their hurt is real and valid and that God sees them, even in their brokenness.

Empathy also involves being patient. Healing from church abuse is not a quick journey, and it often takes longer than we want it to. As you minister to others, remember that healing is a process. It requires time, gentleness, and God's timing. Do not pressure them to "move on" or to stop feeling the way they do. Instead, remind them that God is with them in every step of their journey. Ministering with wisdom means understanding that there is no formula for healing. Each person's story is unique, and each person will walk through the process of healing differently. In Galatians 6:2, Paul writes,

"Carry each other's burdens, and in this way you will fulfil the law of Christ."

This verse speaks directly to the call to support others. Carrying someone's burden does not mean solving their problems or fixing their pain; it means standing with them, listening to them, and offering God's comfort through your presence. Your ministry is not about offering answers but offering a safe space for people to heal.

When ministering to others who have experienced church abuse, one of the most important lessons is not repeating the harmful patterns that caused the hurt in the first place. This might seem obvious, but it is easy to fall into the trap of thinking, "I would never do that," without realizing that we can unintentionally perpetuate the very things that wounded us. The church can be a place of healing, but it can also be a place where toxic patterns are passed down from one generation to the next. As someone who has been hurt, you now have the responsibility to break those cycles.

One of the most common harmful patterns in abusive church settings is the misuse of authority. We've seen leaders who misuse their power to control, manipulate, and dominate others, often under the guise of spiritual authority. But God's idea of authority is rooted in servanthood, not control. In Mark 10:42-45, Jesus teaches His disciples about true leadership: *"Whoever wants to become great among you must be your servant, and whoever wants to be first must be slave of all."* Jesus did not rule with power or intimidation. He led by serving. If you are in a position of leadership or influence, it is crucial to remember this principle: your role is to serve, not to dominate.

This also means that you must be aware of how you exercise authority in your relationships. If you have been wounded by abuse, it can be easy to take on a "better-than-thou" attitude or to misuse your newfound power in an effort to protect yourself. Instead, focus on humility and gentleness. As Paul writes in Philippians 2:3,

"Do nothing out of selfish ambition or vain conceit. Rather, in humility value others above yourselves."

This is the opposite of the manipulative behavior that leads to abuse. Humility allows you to serve others without taking advantage of them.

A harmful pattern that we must avoid is silencing people's voices. Many church abuse victims have experienced the pain of being ignored, dismissed, or silenced. As a healer, you must give others the space to speak, share their pain, and process their emotions. Do not shut down their feelings or try to offer quick answers. Listen carefully, without judgment. Proverbs 18:13 says, *"To answer before listening, that is folly and shame."* Listening well is not just about hearing the words; it is about listening with your heart and giving people the freedom to express themselves fully. Sometimes, the most healing thing you can do is simply to listen.

Be mindful of repeating the cycle of performance-based spirituality. Many people who have been hurt by church have internalized the idea that they must always be "on", always performing, always pleasing, and always serving. This kind of mindset leads to burnout, resentment, and unhealthy expectations. Ministry that heals It does not demand perfection; it invites people to come as they are and find rest. In Matthew 11:28, Jesus calls to the weary, saying, *"Come to me, all you who are weary and burdened, and I will give you rest."* A ministry that offers rest, grace, and acceptance is a ministry that breaks harmful patterns.

Now let's look at how to minister to others in a safe, Christ like way. Healthy, Christ like ministry is about offering hope, comfort, and healing, without manipulating or controlling. It is about leading others into freedom, not into bondage. As you minister to those who have suffered from church abuse, there are a few principles you can follow to ensure that your ministry remains safe and life-giving.

The first principle is to be rooted in love. In 1 Corinthians 13, Paul describes love as patient, kind, and not self-seeking. Love does not take advantage of others or seek its own gain. It is the foundation of all ministry. As you minister to others, make sure that everything you do is rooted in love. Love listens, love supports, and love brings healing. If you are not acting out of love, then you are not ministering as Christ would.

Second, a Christ like ministry prioritizes healing over performance. It is not about getting people to jump through hoops, join programs, or "get over it" quickly. It is about walking alongside people, creating a safe space where they can heal at their own pace. Jesus was never in a rush. He took His time with people. He did not demand that the woman at the well fix herself before He spoke to her; He met her where she was. Similarly, you should offer others the same grace and patience.

Another important principle is to offer accountability, but with gentleness. Christlikeness does not mean ignoring sin or failing to hold people accountable. However, it does mean holding people accountable with kindness and gentleness. Galatians 6:1 says,

"Brothers and sisters, if someone is caught in a sin, you who live by the Spirit should restore that person gently. But watch yourselves, or you also may be tempted."

This kind of accountability does not crush people with guilt; it lifts them up, helping them find restoration and freedom.

Beloved, Christ like ministry is rooted in truth. Truth is not about condemning or shaming; it is about revealing God's heart for healing and wholeness. Ministry that leads to healing always points people to the truth of God's love, the truth of their worth in Christ, and the truth of the hope they have in Him.

Essentially, ministering to others who have suffered church abuse is a sacred responsibility. It requires humility, empathy, and wisdom. It requires a commitment to breaking harmful cycles and establishing a ministry rooted in love, grace, and truth. When you minister from a healed heart, you become a vessel of God's healing, a beacon of hope for others who are still on their journey to wholeness.

Chapter Seventeen:

Healing The Pulpit: Restoration For Wounded Leaders

Leaders Who Are Prisoners of Their Own Wounds

Leadership is often seen as a position of strength, where one is expected to guide, direct, and care for others. But what happens when the leader is themselves wounded? When the one who is supposed to lead others to healing is unable to heal themselves? Unfortunately, many leaders are prisoners of their own wounds, leading from brokenness rather than wholeness. This creates a cycle of hurt and dysfunction that often spills over into the lives of those they lead.

The truth is, unhealed trauma does not just disappear. It hides in the shadows of the heart and shapes everything we do, even our leadership. For a leader, their wounds may show up in their decisions, interactions, and the way they respond to the needs of others. What was once a source of pain can easily become a source of power if left unchecked, manipulating others in subtle but dangerous ways.

Many leaders who have been hurt do not even realize how deeply their wounds affect their leadership. The desire to protect themselves, to control situations, or to avoid vulnerability may come from a place of insecurity and fear. In many cases, the same leader who demands loyalty, respect, and obedience from others may struggle to trust anyone themselves.

"Above all else, guard your heart, for everything you do flows from it"

(Proverbs 4:23, NIV).

The heart of a leader, full of wounds, insecurities, and unresolved pain, affects everything that flows out of them, including their leadership.

Wounded leaders often feel the pressure to perform. They may try to prove their worth by being the "strong" one, always on the go, never showing weakness. They might avoid dealing with their own pain because they believe that leadership requires perfection. But this leads to burnout, cynicism, and even further abuse of those they lead. As you can imagine, such leaders become prisoners of their own wounds, unable to break free and unable to truly help those under their care.

Jesus, in His own ministry, was not a stranger to pain. He understood what it was like to be misunderstood, rejected, and betrayed. However, He did not allow His wounds to control Him. Instead, He allowed His brokenness to be the very place where healing flowed out to others.

"The Spirit of the Sovereign Lord is on me, because the Lord has anointed me to proclaim good news to the poor. He has sent me to bind up the brokenhearted"

(Isaiah 61:1, NIV).

Jesus' wounds were a doorway to healing, not just for Him, but for everyone around Him. This is the call for every leader: to allow God to heal their wounds so that they can be a source of healing for others.

Insecurity is one of the most insidious forces that can shape a leader's behavior. When a leader is insecure, they often lead from a place of fear, rather than from a place of confidence in God. Insecurity in leadership can take many forms: fear of being criticized, fear of failure, and fear of being unappreciated. But no matter what form it takes, insecurity distorts the leader's ability to lead with clarity, grace, and wisdom.

Insecure leaders often struggle with control. They may micromanage, make all the decisions themselves, or demand unquestioning loyalty from their followers. This is because they fear losing power, or they fear that their worth is tied to their performance and the approval of others. They are, in a sense, trying to protect themselves from their own fears and inadequacies, but in doing so, they harm those they lead. Instead of empowering others to grow and take initiative, they stifle their voices and gifs. When insecurity rules a leader's heart, they often look for external validation. They seek approval from people, from the size of the congregation, or from outward signs of success. But true leadership, as Jesus taught, does not depend on external accolades or validation.

"For what is exalted among men is an abomination in the sight of God"

(Luke 16:15, ESV).

The validation that leaders seek should not come from the applause of people but from the approval of God. This does not mean a leader should ignore the concerns of their congregation, but it does mean that their sense of worth should be rooted in God's love for them, not in their performance. The apostle Paul, in 2 Corinthians 12:9-10, writes,

"But he said to me, 'My grace is sufficient for you, for my power is made perfect in weakness.' Therefore I will boast all the more gladly of my weaknesses, so that the power of Christ may rest upon me."

Paul learnt to embrace his weaknesses, and in doing so, he found strength. Insecurity often leads to an outward display of strength, but true strength comes when a leader embraces their brokenness, knowing that God's grace is enough.

The first step toward healing for any leader is to face their brokenness truthfully. Too often, leaders hide behind their titles, their roles, and their positions, refusing to confront the wounds that are impacting their leadership. But the truth is that until a leader is willing to admit their own pain and brokenness, they cannot fully experience healing.

A leader who refuses to acknowledge their wounds is like a house with a leaky roof that refuses to repair the damage. Eventually, the leaks will spread, causing further destruction. The same is true for a leader who refuses to deal with their own brokenness. The wounds will continue to affect their leadership and the people they lead. But when a leader faces their brokenness, admits their need for healing, and seeks help, they begin to take the first step toward true restoration.

In Psalm 51:17, David confesses to God, *"The sacrifices of God are a broken spirit; a broken and contrite heart, O God, you will not despise."* David understood that God does not despise brokenness. He honors it. When a leader humbly comes before God, acknowledging their brokenness and need for healing, God is faithful to restore them.

Leaders who face their brokenness truthfully are not weak; they are strong. They are strong because they are willing to admit that they need God. They are willing to be vulnerable, and vulnerability is where God's strength can truly shine. Leaders, like everyone else, need to allow God to heal their wounds before they can fully lead others into healing.

This does not mean that the healing process is instantaneous. It is ongoing. But facing your brokenness is the first step in that healing journey. As you allow God to tend to your wounds, you will begin to see your leadership flourish in ways you never imagined.

How God Rescues Shepherds Who Mismanage His Flock

One of the most powerful and tender aspects of God's character is His mercy. It is easy for us, as humans, to write off those who fail or mismanage their responsibilities. When leaders make mistakes, especially in the church, the consequences can be devastating. People get hurt, trust is broken, and the very foundation of a ministry can be shaken. But God's mercy is not contingent on perfection; it is poured out for the broken, the failing, and the flawed.

God's mercy toward failing leaders is rooted in His unchanging love. He is not like humans who give up when someone falls short. In the Bible, we see countless examples of leaders who fell, some spectacularly, but were never abandoned by God. Instead, He met them in their brokenness and offered them restoration.

Take the story of King David, for instance. David was called "a man after God's own heart" (Acts 13:22), yet he failed. He committed adultery with Bathsheba, orchestrated her husband's death, and then tried to cover up his sin. If anyone had reason to be discarded by God, it was David. And yet, God showed him incredible mercy. After David's sin was exposed, he did not just apologies; he genuinely repented, acknowledging his wrongdoing before God. In Psalm 51, David cries out, *"Have mercy on me, O God, according to your unfailing love; according to your great compassion blot out my transgressions"* (Psalm 51:1, NIV). God, in His mercy, forgave David and restored him to his place as king. His failure did not define him; God's mercy and forgiveness did.

Similarly, Jesus did not abandon Peter when he denied Him three times. Instead, after His resurrection, Jesus met Peter on the shore, cooked him breakfast, and asked him, *"Do you love me?"* (John 21:15). Three times, Peter affirms his love, and Jesus commissions him to *"Feed my sheep."* Jesus' mercy toward Peter did not just restore him; it also gave him a new calling and purpose. God's mercy toward failing leaders is transformative; it does not just forgive; it renews, refines, and redefines.

When leaders fail, there is often a sense that everything is lost, that the damage is irreparable. But God does not restore through abandonment; He restores through redemption. His goal is not to discard leaders who make mistakes but to bring them back into alignment with His purpose. This is one of the most beautiful aspects of God's restorative work: He does not leave His servants to flounder in failure but works tirelessly to restore order in their lives and ministries.

Restoring order after failure is not the same as pretending nothing happened. God does not simply erase the consequences of poor decisions; He works within those consequences to bring about His redemptive purpose. This is evident in the story of King Saul. Saul's disobedience led to his rejection as king, and yet God did not abandon him outright. Saul's rejection was a result of his own choices, but even then, God continued to give him opportunities to repent and turn back to Him.

In 1 Samuel 16:14, we see the painful moment when "the Spirit of the Lord departed from Saul." God's presence was no longer with him, but that did not mean God was finished with him. In fact, God allowed Saul to continue reigning, even though he had failed. However, when Saul continued to harden his heart, God removed him and raised up David. Despite this, God did not abandon Saul; He still extended His mercy. Later, in 1 Samuel 28, God gave Saul a moment of guidance through a medium (though Saul had gone to a place of spiritual confusion, God still allowed His voice to reach him). While Saul's story is tragic, it highlights how God works within our failures, never abandoning us, but showing us the way forward if we're willing to repent and listen.

God's restoration process does not necessarily look like a complete return to the previous order. In Saul's case, the order of leadership was altered, but God still worked through David, who was able to restore His kingdom. In the same way, when leaders fail, God may raise up new leadership to bring order, but He always invites the fallen leader into a place of humility, repentance, and grace. God does not throw His servants away when they fail. Instead, He gives them opportunities to come back, offering them a new beginning.

The process of restoration for any leader who has failed or mismanaged God's flock involves three key elements: repentance, healing, and transformation. These are not quick fixes; they are ongoing processes that require time, humility, and a willingness to submit to God's work. But when these steps are followed, the result is nothing short of miraculous.

Repentance is the first step in the healing process. Repentance is not just about feeling sorry for what has been done; it is about turning away from the old patterns, attitudes, and behaviors that led to the failure. It is a change of heart and mind that leads to a change in direction. In 2 Samuel 12:13, after the prophet Nathan confronted David about his sin, David responded with a simple but profound admission: *"I have sinned against the Lord."* This is the heart of repentance, a willingness to own up to wrongdoing and turn back to God with a heart of humility.

Repentance isn't just a one-time act; it is a continual posture of turning back to God. Leaders, like everyone else, need to stay humble before God, constantly repenting when they fall short. True repentance involves a broken spirit and a contrite heart, as David said in Psalm 51:17, *"The sacrifices of God are a broken spirit; a broken and contrite heart, O God, you will not despise."* It is through this humility that healing can begin.

Healing is the next step. When leaders have mismanaged God's flock, it is not just their ministry that needs healing; it is their hearts. They need to allow God to heal the wounds that caused the failure in the first place. Sometimes these wounds are rooted in insecurity, fear, or unmet needs that the leader has been carrying. If not dealt with, these wounds can lead to unhealthy leadership practices, such as control, manipulation, or neglect. In Jeremiah 30:17, God promises to heal His people, saying,

"But I will restore you to health and heal your wounds,' declares the Lord."

Healing for leaders is about returning to God's heart, receiving His mercy, and allowing Him to mend what has been broken. Leaders who have experienced failure need to allow themselves to be healed by God's loving touch before they can effectively lead others into healing.

Transformation is the final step in the restoration process. True restoration does not just involve going back to the way things were before. It involves a transformation of heart, mind, and leadership style. When God restores a leader, He does not just put a fresh coat of paint over old, broken walls; He transforms the leader into someone new, someone who leads with humility, grace, and a heart for service. In Romans 12:2, Paul writes,

"Do not conform to the pattern of this world, but be transformed by the renewing of your mind. Then you will be able to test and approve what God's will is, His good, pleasing, and perfect will."

This is the transformation that every leader needs: a renewal of mind that leads to a transformation of heart. God changes how leaders think about their role, how they view their followers, and how they approach their ministry. Instead of leading from a place of insecurity and fear, they learn to lead from a place of peace, grace, and love.

Thus, when God rescues shepherds who have mismanaged His flock, He does so with mercy, compassion, and patience. He does not abandon His servants; He restores them through repentance, healing, and transformation. God's heart is always to redeem, to restore, and to equip leaders to lead in ways that honors Him and nurture His people. When a leader is willing to face their brokenness, allow God to heal their wounds, and submit to His transformative work, they become the kind of leader who can guide others with humility, grace, and wisdom.

Chapter Eighteen:

Healing The Congregation: Restoring Unity And Love

Deliverance from Toxic Culture in The Church

A toxic church culture can be one of the most damaging environments for believers. It eats away at the very essence of what church is meant to be: community, healing, and spiritual growth. When the culture within a church becomes poisoned by unhealthy behavior, toxic leadership, gossip, judgment, or division, it creates an atmosphere where people feel unsafe, unsupported, and even unwanted. In such an environment, the very purpose of the church, being the body of Christ, is lost. Instead of being a place of refuge, it becomes a place of harm, where those who enter in search of healing find only more wounds.

But here is the hope: God has a plan to bring deliverance to His church. He has called His people to be a community of love, humility, and grace, and it is possible for even the most toxic church cultures to be healed. The first step is identifying the root behaviors that create such an environment. Once we can see what's causing the poison, we can begin the work of uprooting it and cultivating a culture that reflects Christ's love.

The root of a toxic church culture can be traced back to several key behaviors that perpetuate harm. One of the most common is the misuse of authority. When leaders abuse their power, whether by manipulating, controlling, or demanding blind obedience, it creates an atmosphere of fear and distrust. This unhealthy dynamic keeps people from experiencing the freedom and love that the gospel offers. Instead, they are bound by fear, where love is conditional, and obedience is coerced.

Jesus warned against such leadership in Matthew 23:4, where He said,

"They tie up heavy, cumbersome loads and put them on other people's shoulders, but they themselves are not willing to lift a finger to move them."

(NIV).

Leaders who use their position to control others instead of nurturing them create a toxic environment that leaves people feeling burdened and trapped, rather than loved and supported.

Another toxic behavior is gossip. When members of the congregation engage in gossip, spreading rumors, criticizing, or talking about others behind their backs, trust is broken. Gossip breeds division, and before long, factions begin to form. This creates a hostile environment where people no longer feel safe. Proverbs 16:28 tells us,

"A perverse person stirs up conflict, and a gossip separates close friends."

(NIV).

Gossip is one of the most destructive forces in the church because it spreads division and mistrust, making it difficult for people to feel like they belong to a united body.

Judgment and comparison are also major contributors to a toxic church culture. When people are constantly judged or compared to others, they begin to feel inadequate and unworthy. This spirit of comparison, where one person's worth is measured against another's, stifles growth and creates a culture of competition rather than cooperation. In James 2:1, the apostle James warns against favoritism, saying, *"My brothers and sisters, believers in our glorious Lord Jesus Christ must not show* favoritism." (NIV). A church where comparison and judgment reign is not a place where people can truly grow and flourish.

Once we've identified these toxic behaviors, the next step is uprooting them. This is not easy work, especially if these behaviors have been ingrained over time. A dysfunctional church culture does not change overnight. It requires intentional, consistent effort from both leadership and the congregation. However, with God's guidance, healing is possible.

The first step in uprooting dysfunction is repentance. Repentance is a biblical concept that means turning away from sin and turning toward God. In a toxic church, this means acknowledging the ways in which harmful behaviors have been allowed to persist, whether in leadership or among members. It is about admitting that the culture has become unhealthy and asking God for forgiveness and transformation. In 2 Chronicles 7:14, God promises,

"If my people, who are called by my name, will humble themselves and pray and seek my face and turn from their wicked ways, then I will hear from heaven, and I will forgive their sin and will heal their land."

(NIV).

God offers healing to His people when they genuinely repent, not just for their actions but for the unhealthy culture that has taken root.

Once repentance has occurred, the next step is to establish new patterns. A healthy church culture requires intentionality in fostering love, grace, and humility. The apostle Paul encourages the church in Ephesians 4:2-3,

"Be completely humble and gentle; be patient, bearing with one another in love. Make every effort to keep the unity of the Spirit through the bond of peace."

(NIV).

This calls for a radical shift from a culture of comparison, judgment, and control to one of humility, patience, and mutual support. Leaders need to model humility, serve others, and make efforts to build unity. Congregants must learn to bear with one another, showing grace and love even when disagreements arise.

Another important step in uprooting toxicity is creating a space for honest conversations. People in toxic environments often feel silenced or fearful of speaking up. But for healing to begin, there needs to be room for people to voice their concerns, frustrations, and hopes for the church. This can be difficult, but it is necessary. In James 5:16, we are encouraged to

"Confess your sins to each other and pray for each other so that you may be healed."

(NIV).

Healing does not happen in isolation. It happens in community, when people are able to be honest and vulnerable with each other.

Prayer is also a vital part of uprooting long-standing dysfunctional patterns. Only God can bring true transformation to a toxic culture. When the church pray together, seeking God's wisdom and guidance, He will lead them into unity and love. In 1 Timothy 2:1-2, Paul encourages prayer for everyone, including leaders: "I urge, then, first of all, that petitions, prayers, intercession and thanksgiving be made for all people, for kings and all those in authority, that we may live peaceful and quiet lives."

Building A House Where Grace Lives Again

A grace-filled community is the kind of church that every believer longs for. It is a place where healing happens, where relationships are nurtured, and where people feel safe to be themselves, flaws and all. Grace is not just a theological concept in a grace-filled community; it is the atmosphere that permeates every interaction, every sermon, every prayer, and every shared moment. This grace does not dismiss sin or pretend that everything is perfect. Rather, it invites people to experience God's unconditional love, not based on what they do, but on who He is.

A grace-filled community looks like a place where people are allowed to grow at their own pace, without judgment or condemnation. The church, as the body of Christ, should be a place where love is the driving force behind all actions. In John 13:34-35, Jesus tells His disciples,

"A new command I give you: Love one another. As I have loved you, so you must love one another. By this everyone will know that you are my disciples, if you love one another."

(NIV).

Love in a grace-filled church is not a superficial, feel-good sentiment; it is active, sacrificial, and unconditional. It means standing with people in their darkest moments, forgiving them when they've wronged us, and walking alongside them as they heal.

The church must also be a place where forgiveness is the norm. In a grace-filled community, people do not hold grudges, and they do not keep a record of wrongs. When someone sins or hurts another, the response is not anger or exclusion but a willingness to forgive and restore. In Colossians 3:13, Paul encourages the church to

"Bear with each other and forgive one another if any of you has a grievance against someone. Forgive as the Lord forgave you."

(NIV).

A grace-filled community is one where people forgive quickly and completely, understanding that they too have been forgiven much by God.

In a grace-filled community, there is also freedom. Freedom to be imperfect. Freedom to stumble. Freedom to ask questions and doubt. The atmosphere is one of non-judgmental support, where spiritual growth is embraced and nurtured, and where the pressure to perform or meet unrealistic standards is replaced with the gentle invitation of grace. In Matthew 11:28-30, Jesus calls all who are weary and burdened,

"Come to me, all you who are weary and burdened, and I will give you rest. Take my yoke upon you and learn from me, for I am gentle and humble in heart, and you will find rest for your souls."

(NIV).

A grace-filled community is one that follows Christ's example of gentleness, offering rest and peace to those who are struggling.

Rebuilding trust and unity in a congregation that has been damaged by toxicity requires intentional practices that promote openness, honesty, and healing. Trust is the foundation of any healthy relationship, and in the church, it must be nurtured with care and consistency. It cannot be rushed or forced. It must be built slowly, brick by brick, with every word spoken, every action taken, and every relationship restored.

One of the first practices in rebuilding trust is transparency. People need to know that they can trust their leaders and fellow members to be honest with them. Transparency begins with the leaders themselves. Leaders must model openness, even about their own weaknesses and struggles. In James 5:16, we are reminded, *"Therefore confess your sins to each other and pray for each other so that you may be healed."* (NIV). This does not mean airing out personal issues to everyone, but it does mean creating a culture where authenticity is valued and where it is safe to admit that we do not have it all together. When leaders model vulnerability and honesty, it creates a space for others to do the same.

In rebuilding trust, active listening is important. Listening is one of the simplest yet most profound ways to rebuild unity in a congregation. When people feel heard, they feel valued. And when they feel valued, trust grows. In a grace-filled community, people should not only listen to others with empathy but also listen to God. This involves creating spaces where individuals feel free to share their concerns, ideas, and even complaints without fear of being dismissed or reprimanded. The church should also practice reconciliation. Jesus taught us in Matthew 5:23-24 that if we have anything against someone, we should go to them and be reconciled.

"Therefore, if you are offering your gift at the altar and there remember that your brother or sister has something against you, leave your gift there in front of the altar. First go and be reconciled to them; then come and offer your gift."

(NIV).

Reconciliation isn't just about fixing relationships; it is about restoring harmony, peace, and unity. In a healthy church, members should be encouraged to reconcile with each other when conflict arises. This practice helps prevent division and fosters a sense of unity, ensuring that the body of Christ remains whole.

A healthy church will create opportunities for shared experiences that build community and trust. This could be through small groups, service projects, or events that bring people together outside of Sunday services. Acts 2:44-47 describes the early church, saying, "All the believers were together and had everything in common. They sold property and possessions to give to anyone who had need. Every day they continued to meet together in the temple courts. They broke bread in their homes and ate together with glad and sincere hearts.

Chapter Nineteen:

Deliverance From Religious Captivity

Breaking Invisible Chains of Manipulation, Control And Shame

Have you ever felt trapped in an invisible prison? A prison built not of walls, but of chains of manipulation, control, and shame that seem to follow you wherever you go. For many, this prison is spiritual. They are bound not by physical barriers but by oppressive, controlling systems disguised as religious authority. It is a reality many believers face: manipulative teachings, shame-based leadership, and distorted doctrines that create a sense of bondage rather than freedom in Christ.

These invisible chains can affect every area of life, how we think, how we feel, and how we relate to God and others. We may find ourselves caught in cycles of fear, doubt, and shame, constantly measuring our worth by unattainable standards, believing lies about God's love and our own value. But God did not call us to live in captivity; He called us to freedom.

The first step to breaking free from spiritual captivity is recognizing the chains that hold us. These chains are often subtle, working their way into our hearts and minds over time. The chains of manipulation and control are most often hidden behind what seems like "spiritual authority". Church leaders, who are meant to shepherd, can sometimes distort their position and demand obedience based on fear, guilt, or shame rather than love.

Manipulation in religious systems often comes disguised as spiritual guidance. It is the leader who uses fear of punishment or eternal damnation to control behavior or who places themselves between you and God, making it feel as though you can only hear from God through them. This kind of manipulation keeps you dependent on the leader instead of on God's Word and His direct relationship with you. It is a tactic straight from the enemy, using God's name to create dependence and control.

Shame is another keychain that binds believers. Shame-based teaching often makes people feel unworthy, broken, or incapable of truly experiencing God's love and forgiveness. It is the belief that you must constantly strive to prove yourself to God, that you must earn His love and approval. But this is not the gospel. *"There is now no condemnation for those who are in Christ Jesus"* (Romans 8:1, NIV). The gospel tells us that we are not defined by our past mistakes or by any spiritual leader's judgment. We are free because of Christ's finished work on the cross.

Another form of bondage is spiritual abuse, where a leader uses their authority to manipulate or control the emotions of their followers. These leaders may play on the guilt and vulnerability of their congregants, making them feel obligated to perform or behave a certain way to remain in good standing. In 1 Peter 5:3, the apostle Peter warns, *"Not lording it over those entrusted to you, but being examples to the flock"* (NIV). Spiritual authority should never be used to manipulate or coerce; it should be used to guide, encourage, and help others grow closer to God.

The chains of spiritual bondage do not just affect our actions; they affect our thoughts and our worldview. When we're trapped in a system that manipulates and controls, our minds are clouded by lies and fear. We start to believe that we're not good enough for God's love, that we have to perform to be worthy, or that God is angry with us when we fall short. These distorted thoughts influence our behavior, causing us to make decisions out of fear, guilt, or shame rather than love and grace.

For instance, the lie that we must earn God's favor can lead us into a cycle of striving. We may feel compelled to do more, be more, and serve more to prove that we're worthy of God's love. But this is not what the Bible teaches. In Ephesians 2:8-9, Paul reminds us,

"For it is by grace you have been saved, through faith, and this is not from yourselves; it is the gift of God, not by works, so that no one can boast."

(NIV).

This truth breaks the chain of self-performance. You do not need to work for God's love; He gives it freely.

Spiritual bondage also affects the way we see ourselves. We can begin to view ourselves as failures, unworthy, or unlovable. These thoughts infiltrate our relationship with God, making it difficult to approach Him with confidence. But the truth is, God sees us as His beloved children, accepted and cherished.

"See what great love the Father has lavished on us, that we should be called children of God!"

(1 John 3:1, NIV).

When we see ourselves through God's eyes, we can begin to break free from the lies that have held us captive.

The negative effects of spiritual bondage also affect our behavior. We may start to perform for others, seeking validation and approval from people instead of God. We may avoid taking risks or stepping into our true calling because we fear failure or rejection. But this is not how God wants us to live. He calls us to walk in the freedom He has given us through Christ:

"It is for freedom that Christ has set us free. Stand firm, then, and do not let yourselves be burdened again by a yoke of slavery" (Galatians 5:1, NIV).

Tools for Breaking Free Through Truth And Discernment

The key to breaking free from spiritual bondage is truth, God's truth. The truth is that you are loved unconditionally, that you are accepted by God, and that you do not have to earn His love or approval. *"Then you will know the truth, and the truth will set you free"* (John 8:32, NIV). When you begin to embrace the truth of God's Word, the chains that bind you begin to loosen. The lies you've believed are replaced with the truth of who you are in Christ.

One of the most powerful tools for breaking free is spiritual discernment. Discernment helps you recognize the lies and false teachings that have kept you in bondage. It helps you distinguish between the voice of the enemy and the voice of God. In 1 John 4:1, we are instructed to *"test the spirits to see whether they are from God, because many false prophets have gone out into the world."* (NIV). Discernment allows you to evaluate what you are hearing, whether from church leaders, teachings, or your own thoughts, and compare it with the truth of Scripture.

Another key tool is community. It is difficult to break free from spiritual bondage alone. We need others to help us see the truth, encourage us, and walk with us as we heal. In Hebrews 10:24-25, the writer encourages believers to "Consider how we may spur one another on toward love and good deeds, not giving up meeting together, as some are in the habit of doing, but encouraging one another."

Restoration Of Joy, Faith, And Spiritual Freedom

Pain is an inevitable part of life. It is the price of living in a broken world. But just because pain is part of the journey does not mean that joy has to be absent. For many who have suffered, whether from church hurt, personal loss, or spiritual oppression, joy can feel like a distant memory, something that once was but has now slipped beyond reach. The good news is that God specializes in restoring joy. Not a fleeting happiness based on circumstances, but a deep, abiding joy that transcends pain.

Rediscovering joy after seasons of pain begins with acknowledging that it is okay to mourn. There is no shame in feeling sad, hurt, or broken. In fact, the Bible encourages us to be honest with God about our pain. *"The Lord is close to the brokenhearted and saves those who are crushed in spirit"* (Psalm 34:18, NIV). God is not afraid of our emotions. He does not expect us to pretend everything is okay when it is not. The first step toward joy is to allow yourself to feel the weight of your pain, to cry when you need to, and to acknowledge the wounds you carry.

However, the key to rediscovering joy is not staying in the pain. God does not leave us there. He does not allow us to remain stuck in sorrow or despair. Psalm 30:5 says,

"Weeping may stay for the night, but rejoicing comes in the morning"

(NIV).

Joy does not come instantly, but it does come. Just as the sun rises after a dark night, so too does joy rise after seasons of suffering. The process may take time, but God promises that morning will come. And when it does, it is more than just a glimpse of happiness; it is a deep joy that only He can provide.

This joy is not dependent on external circumstances. It is a joy that springs up from knowing that, despite everything, God is still with us. *"The joy of the Lord is your strength"* (Nehemiah 8:10, NIV). When we rediscover God's presence, we rediscover joy. This joy does not deny the pain, but it holds onto the truth that God's love is greater than anything we face. This joy is an anchor for the soul, a strength that enables us to keep moving forward even in the toughest of times.

How God Restores Vibrant Faith

Faith is the bedrock of the Christian life. It is what sustains us in times of trial and gives us hope for the future. But when we've been wounded, especially spiritually, our faith can begin to feel shaky, fragile, or even non-existent. We may find ourselves questioning God's goodness, wondering if He is truly trustworthy. But God, in His mercy and grace, is able to restore vibrant faith.

The process of restoring faith begins with remembering who God is. When we've been hurt, it is easy to focus on our circumstances and lose sight of God's nature. We begin to define God by our experiences, rather than by His Word. The truth is, God is always good, always faithful, and always present, whether we feel it or not. In 2 Timothy 2:13, Paul reminds us, *"If we are faithless, he remains faithful, for he cannot deny himself"* (ESV). God's faithfulness does not depend on our performance. Even in our doubts and struggles, He remains the same. His goodness is constant. To restore our faith, we need to refocus on God's promises. In Romans 10:17, Paul writes,

"Faith comes from hearing the message, and the message is heard through the word about Christ"

(NIV).

God's Word is the foundation of our faith. When we immerse ourselves in Scripture, we are reminded of who God is and what He has promised. His Word strengthens our faith, just as food strengthens the body. If you've been spiritually wounded, begin by reading the promises of God in the Bible. Let His Word renew your mind and restore your heart.

It is also important to remember that faith is a journey. It is not about reaching perfection in our belief but about trusting God one step at a time. The father in Mark 9:24 cried out, *"I do believe; help me overcome my unbelief!"* (NIV). This is the heart of restored faith, acknowledging our doubts and bringing them to God. He does not require perfect faith; He requires a willing heart that is open to His healing power. So, take it one day at a time. Trust Him with small steps, and watch as He builds your faith.

Another key to restoring vibrant faith is remembering that faith is relational, not transactional. We often think of faith as something we "use" to get what we want from God, but in reality, faith is about knowing and trusting God. It is about walking with Him, even when we do not understand His ways. In Matthew 17:20, Jesus said,

"If you have faith as small as a mustard seed, you can say to this mountain, 'Move from here to there,' and it will move. Nothing will be impossible for you"

(NIV).

Faith, even in small amounts, can move mountains. It is not about the size of our faith but the object of our faith, God Himself. And when we trust Him, our faith grows stronger and more vibrant.

Restoration is a process, and while we may experience breakthroughs and healing, the challenge comes in protecting that newfound freedom. It is easy to fall back into old patterns, old lies, and unhealthy behaviors. But when God restores your joy and faith, He also gives you the responsibility to protect it. Freedom requires vigilance.

You must protect your mind. In 2 Corinthians 10:5, Paul writes,

"We demolish arguments and every pretension that sets itself up against the knowledge of God, and we take captive every thought to make it obedient to Christ"

(NIV).

Your thoughts are powerful. If you allow negative thoughts, doubts, or lies to take root, they can undo the healing God has done in you. Be mindful of what you allow to linger in your mind. When negative or false thoughts arise, replace them with God's truth. Guard your thoughts like precious treasure, and do not allow the enemy to steal your peace.

You must also protect your environment. You've likely encountered the saying, "You become like the people you spend time with." It is true. If you want to protect the freedom God has given you, be intentional about the people you surround yourself with. Find people who will encourage you, pray with you, and walk alongside you in your healing journey. In Proverbs 13:20, Solomon wisely says, *"Walk with the wise and become wise, for a companion of fools suffers harm"* (NIV). Healthy relationships are a safeguard for your freedom. Surround yourself with people who will speak life into you and hold you accountable in love.

Also, protect your time. Protecting your newfound freedom also means protecting your time with God. In Mark 1:35, we see Jesus retreating early in the morning to pray and spend time with the Father. If Jesus, the Son of God, needed time with the Father, how much more do we need it? Your time with God is what keeps you grounded in His truth. Do not let the busyness of life steal away your time in His presence. Make it a priority to nurture your relationship with God through prayer, worship, and the study of His Word.

Protect your freedom by living intentionally. Do not take the healing God has given you for granted. Instead, use it to grow, to serve, and to glorify God. Your freedom in Christ is a gift, and it is worth fighting for.

Chapter Twenty:

A New Kind Of Church: The Healing Community

What A Christ like, Healthy Church Looks Like

When we think about the church, we should imagine a place that reflects the character and love of Christ. A Christ like church is not just a gathering of believers; it is a living embodiment of God's Kingdom on Earth. It is a place where the broken find healing, where the lost are found, and where the hurting are restored. But what does a truly Christ like church look like?

The first characteristic of a Christ like church is love. Jesus told His disciples that the world would know they were His followers by their love for one another. In John 13:34-35, He says,

"A new command I give you: Love one another. As I have loved you, so you must love one another. By this, everyone will know that you are my disciples if you love one another."

(NIV).

Love is not just a feeling; it is an action, a lifestyle. A healthy church is one where love is not just a theory we talk about but a practice we live out daily. Love looks like forgiveness, compassion, patience, and kindness. It means we show grace to each other in our weaknesses and imperfections. It means we honors one another's dignity, even when we disagree or fall short.

Another defining characteristic of a Christ like church is humility. A healthy church reflects Christ's humility. Philippians 2:5-7 encourages us to have the same mindset as Christ,

"Who, being in very nature God, did not consider equality with God something to be used to his own advantage; rather, he made himself nothing by taking the very nature of a servant, being made in human likeness."

(NIV).

A humble church does not elevate leaders above others. It does not create hierarchies of importance. Instead, it acknowledges that every member of the body is valuable. Humility means that we serve one another, not because we are compelled, but because we choose to. It means we're not concerned with titles, status, or recognition. We're only concerned with living like Christ and serving others selflessly.

A Christ like church also emphasizes healing and restoration. In Luke 4:18, Jesus declares that He was sent *"to proclaim good news to the poor...to proclaim freedom for the prisoners and recovery of sight for the blind, to set the oppressed free."* (NIV). A healthy church is a place where people find freedom from their past, their sins, and their wounds. It is a place where individuals can come as they are and experience true healing spiritually, emotionally, and relationally. A Christ like church is intentional about creating a safe environment for healing to happen. It welcomes the hurting, the broken, and the outcasts without judgment.

A Christ like church is a place of truth. This is not truth that condemns or crushes the spirit, but truth that sets people free. John

8:32 says, *"Then you will know the truth, and the truth will set you free."* (NIV). In a healthy church, truth is shared with love, not as a weapon but as a pathway to freedom. Truth can be difficult, especially when we need to face our shortcomings, but it is always liberating. The church should be a place where we speak the truth in love, challenge each other to grow, and help one another become more like Christ. In a Christ like church, love, humility, healing, and truth create a powerful culture of grace. This is the kind of church we should all long for, one that reflects the heart of Jesus in every way.

Now, let's contrast this vision of a Christ like church with what we often see in abusive church environments. In abusive churches, the culture is centered around power, control, and fear rather than love, humility, and grace. Leaders in abusive environments often manipulate their congregations by using guilt, shame, or fear to keep people in line. Instead of leading by example, they demand blind obedience and obedience out of fear rather than love for God and His people. In contrast, a healthy church leads by humility and love, serving others rather than lording authority over them.

Another stark contrast is in the way people are treated. In abusive churches, there is often an unspoken or even spoken hierarchy where some are valued more than others based on their status or position. Members of the congregation are made to feel insignificant unless they meet certain standards or fulfil certain roles. In a healthy church, however, every individual is valued, regardless of their status or role. There are no "greater" members of the body of Christ; each part is equally important (1 Corinthians 12:14-27).

Whereas abusive churches thrive on secrecy and control, healthy churches thrive on transparency and freedom. Abusive churches foster a culture of fear, where questioning or speaking up is discouraged and even punished. Members are often kept in the dark about important decisions, and those in authority may manipulate information to maintain control. In contrast, a healthy church encourages open communication and transparency. It welcomes questions, values input from members, and operates with integrity.

Perhaps the most significant difference is how people feel when they leave church. In abusive environments, people often feel drained, spiritually dry, and emotionally exhausted. The church becomes a source of anxiety and oppression. On the other hand, in a healthy church, people feel refreshed, energized, and equipped to live out their faith. They leave church with a renewed sense of purpose and joy, knowing that they are loved by God and are part of a community that nurtures their growth.

A healthy church reflects the character of Christ, one of compassion, grace, and mercy. An abusive church reflects the spirit of control and manipulation. The stark differences between these two environments are obvious, but the good news is that healing is possible. God desires to restore His church to its intended state, one that reflects His love, His grace, and His truth.

Now, let's look toward the future with hope. You see, God has a vision for His church, a vision that goes beyond programs, traditions, and buildings. He wants His house to be a place where His people can come together in love, in freedom, and in unity. The church is meant to be a reflection of God's Kingdom on Earth. It should be a place of healing, restoration, and hope for a broken world.

In Revelation 21:3, it says, "And I heard a loud voice from the throne saying, 'Look! God's dwelling place is now among the people, and he will dwell with them. They will be his people, and God himself will be with them and be their God.'" (NIV). This is the vision for God's house: a dwelling place where He is present with His people, guiding them, healing them, and uniting them. A healthy church is not just a building or an institution; it is a community where God's presence is felt, and His love is experienced in real, tangible ways. It is a place where individuals encounter God's transformative power, not just on Sundays, but in every aspect of life.

God desires His house to be a sanctuary, a place where His peace rules, His grace abounds, and His truth is spoken in love. In this space, there are no barriers between people. There is no hierarchy or division. Everyone is welcome, and every person is valued as a unique and beloved member of God's family. Ephesians 2:19-22 says,

"Consequently, you are no longer foreigners and strangers, but fellow citizens with God's people and also members of his household, built on the foundation of the apostles and prophets, with Christ Jesus himself as the chief cornerstone."

(NIV).

A healthy church is built on the foundation of Christ, where each member is connected to Him and to one another as part of the same household.

This is the vision we must pursue: a church where unity and love are not just ideals but the very fabric of the community. A church where healing flows freely, where people can be open about their struggles and find restoration, and where grace is not a concept but a lived reality. This church does not just preach the gospel; it lives it. It does not just teach about love; it practices it. And it does not just talk about healing; it creates an environment where the wounded can come and be made whole.

To create a church where healing and restoration are possible, we must first understand that God's house is meant to be a place of rest. Rest does not just mean physical rest; it is spiritual and emotional rest. It is a place where people can come and find peace in the midst of their pain, strength in the midst of their weakness, and hope in the midst of despair.

When a person walks into a church that is a house of rest, they should feel a sense of security and peace. This peace comes from knowing that they are not judged or condemned for their struggles but welcomed with open arms. The church must be a place where people are allowed to be themselves, where they do not have to hide their wounds or pretend they are perfect. They can come as they are and experience the healing presence of God.

In Matthew 11:28-30, Jesus invites all who are weary and burdened to come to Him for rest: "Come to me, all you who are weary and burdened, and I will give you rest. Take my yoke upon you and learn from me, for I am gentle and humble in heart, and you will find rest for your souls." (NIV). Jesus offers a rest that is different from the world's rest, a rest that does not just relieve physical tiredness but brings peace to the soul. A church that is a house of rest reflects this same heart of Jesus. It is a place where people can find solace, where the healing power of God is tangible, and where the burdens of life are lifted in His presence.

For a church to become a house of rest, it must be intentional about creating a culture of healing. This begins with leadership. Leaders must lead with humility and empathy, understanding the struggles of the congregation and offering compassion. Leaders should also model rest for their people, recognizing that spiritual burnout is real and creating spaces for leaders and members to rest, recharge, and be restored.

A house of rest also nurtures the wounded by encouraging healing through community. Galatians 6:2 urges believers to "Carry each other's burdens, and in this way you will fulfil the law of Christ." (NIV). The church must be a place where people care for one another, where members walk alongside each other in their healing journeys, offering prayer, encouragement, and accountability. No one should have to walk through pain alone. Healing is a community project, and a healthy church fosters this sense of shared responsibility and mutual care.

A healthy church must intentionally create safe spaces for people to grow and heal. These spaces are not just physical places but emotional and spiritual environments where people feel accepted, loved, and free to be vulnerable. A safe space is one where trust is built, where judgment is absent, and where healing can take place without fear of rejection or condemnation.

One of the most important elements of a safe space is confidentiality. People need to know that they can share their struggles without fear that others will gossip or spread rumors. In a healthy church, confidentiality is taken seriously. People's personal journeys, struggles, and prayer requests are handled with care and respect. Leaders must be trustworthy and transparent, and the church must establish guidelines for handling sensitive information.

Another essential element is accountability. A safe space does not mean a space free from accountability. Accountability is vital for growth and healing. However, accountability in a healthy church is done with grace, not judgment. It is done with the understanding that we are all on a journey, and no one is perfect. Accountability is not about condemning or criticizing, but about encouraging one another to grow in faith, holiness, and love.

Furthermore, a safe space encourages vulnerability. People who have been wounded often put up walls to protect themselves, fearing that if they let their guard down, they will be hurt again. A healthy church creates an environment where vulnerability is met with compassion, where people can be honest about their pain, struggles, and doubts without fear of being rejected. The church should be a place where healing is allowed to unfold, and people are given the grace to process their emotions at their own pace.

God's desire is for the church to be a place of healing for the world. The world is broken, hurting, and in need of hope. As believers, we are called to be agents of that hope, bringing healing to a world that desperately needs it. A healing culture in the church is not just for the benefit of its members but for the community at large. When the church becomes a house of rest and restoration, it becomes a beacon of light to the world.

You, as a member of the body of Christ, are called to participate in building this healing culture. It starts with your own healing, your own willingness to embrace God's love and grace. But it does not end there. You are called to help others on their journey, to extend the same love, grace, and healing that you have received. This means being intentional about how you relate to others, how you encourage and support them, and how you help build a community where trust, love, and healing can thrive. In 1 Peter 4:10, Peter writes,

"Each of you should use whatever gift you have received to serve others, as faithful stewards of God's grace in its various forms."

(NIV).

The healing culture you help build will be shaped by the gifts, talents, and love that you bring to the table. You are called to be a steward of God's grace, living it, sharing it, and cultivating it in your church community. The church is meant to be a house where the wounded can find healing, where the broken can find restoration, and where everyone can experience the love and grace of Christ. It is time to become that house. The healing begins with you.

Conclusion

This book has shown you that spiritual pain is not proof of spiritual failure. It is often the cost of sincerity. When you loved deeply, trusted fully, and believed honestly, the betrayal cut deeper. That does not make you weak. It makes you human. And more than that, it makes you reachable by grace. You must understand that you are not broken goods trying to find your way back to God. You were never sent away in the first place. God did not step back when leaders failed, He stepped closer. He did not abandon you in the wilderness, He met you there. What felt like isolation was actually invitation, what felt like loss was preparation.

You now understand that silence can wound, but it can also heal. That authority can be misused, but God's authority always restores. That fear-based faith shrinks the soul, but love-based faith expands it. You have learnt to separate God's heart from human error. That alone is freedom. And here is the one truth you may not have fully realized yet: you are not just healed for yourself. You are healed for others. Every tear you processed instead of suppressing became oil. Every boundary you learnt to honors became wisdom. Every false doctrine you unlearned sharpened your discernment. You now carry something rare: the ability to sit with the wounded without judging them, rushing them, or controlling them. You know how to listen without trying to fix. You know how to speak without manipulating. You know how to point people to God without placing yourself in His place. That is not accidental. That is calling.

As a believer, as a born-again child of God, you are already an ambassador of Christ. Scripture says you carry the ministry of reconciliation. Not because you are perfect, but because you are honest. Not because you are loud, but because you are present. You understand pain in sacred spaces. You recognize trauma hidden behind religious language. You can stand in the gap where others could not.

If you choose to, you can serve as a chaplain in the truest sense of the word, not just officially, but spiritually. A safe presence. A grounded voice. A steady witness to God's gentleness. You are proof that faith can survive disappointment and still remain tender.

You no longer need to perform spirituality to belong. You belong because God chose you. You no longer need permission to heal. Heaven already gave it. You no longer need to fear being sent away from God's presence. You live in it. So carry this new knowledge forward. Let your life testify that God restores without shaming. That He rebuilds without controlling. That He leads without coercion. Let your faith be quiet but unshakeable. Let your compassion be deep but discerning. Let your boundaries be firm and your heart remain soft. You are not returning to who you were before the brethren hurt you. You are becoming who you could not have been without the healing. God is not finished with you rather, He is just getting started.

References

- Challenging narcissistic leaders and toxic cultures. (2025, February 27). Insights Magazine. https://www.insights.uca.org.au/challenging-narcissistic-leaders-and-toxic-cultures/

- Community, F. P. (2025, April 11). Healing from Religious Trauma: Reclaim Your Faith. Faithful Path Community. https://faithfulpathcommunity.com/healing-from-religious-trauma-reclaim-your-faith

- Harrington, G. (2025, June 2). How to forgive church hurt without losing your faith. Ginger Harrington. https://gingerharrington.com/forgive-church-hurt/

- Healing from Spiritual Betrayal and Religious Trauma. (n.d.). Being Real PLLC. https://on-being-real.com/when-faith-betrays-reclaiming-your-voice-after-spiritual-and-psychological-harm

- McConnaughey, J. (2023, December 8). How do fear-based teachings cause religious trauma? Janyne McConnaughey. https://janyne.substack.com/p/how-do-fear-based-teachings-cause-religious-trauma

- Rose, N. (2024, July 16). Restoring my spirituality after years of religious abuse | CPTSDfoundation.org. https://cptsdfoundation.org/2024/07/16/restoring-my-spirituality-after-years-of-religious-abuse/

- Shame is the tool of the enemy – expedition of the soul. (2023, August 28). https://expeditionofthesoul.com/2023/08/28/shame-is-the-tool-of-the-enemy/

- Smith, S. (2012, August 18). A biblical perspective on spiritual authority and critical thinking. Liberty for Captives. https://libertyforcaptives.com/2012/08/17/a-biblical-perspective-on-spiritual-authority-and-critical-thinking/

- Thomas, R. (2024, January 25). Eight signs of spiritual abuse in the church. Life Over Coffee. https://lifeovercoffee.com/a-few-signs-of-spiritual-abuse-from-a-pastor/?srsltid=AfmBOoqJJfOe-BA9WfiIxxYW7wHnaD-1-Y0u9G_-C7eJ7mtiFplCxxne

About The Book

This book is a compassionate but brave guide for people who believe in God but have been hurt by spiritual abuse, teachings based on fear, and misplaced faith. With clarity, compassion and depth from the Bible, it helps you understand God's true heart apart from the failures or inadequacies of humans who may be in positions of influence and leadership over us. Through this book, you will be led out of confusion and into freedom, healing, and a closer relationship with God through the healing insights, scripture, and practical advice. This book does not accuse you; instead, it wakes you up and invites you to rediscover God as He really is and step fearlessly into wholeness, purpose, and spiritual maturity.

About The Author

Sophia Lorraine Wilson is a Personal Support Worker (PSW) who resides permanently in Canada, where she carries out her duties devotedly in hospitals, nursing homes, and within the wider community. She is a dedicated Christian and a committed student of the Word of God. Sophia enjoys giving, singing, and serving in intercessory ministry both at home and in church. She wholeheartedly embraces her care ministry and finds deep fulfillment in outreach, as she genuinely loves people and gives herself fully to the needs of others.

This book, *Church Abuse*, was inspired by the intuition of the Holy Spirit. It serves as a source of clarity and insight, helping readers to see more clearly and to make necessary adjustments as we move forward in reaching the lost for Jesus Christ. As a citizen of the great nation of Canada, Sophia's earnest desire is to see the Church of the Lord Jesus Christ excel in knowledge, wisdom, and understanding.

Sophia is the mother of two sons and two grandchildren. She is a lover of animals and people, and her life aspiration and guiding motto remain, *Nothing is impossible when we put our trust in God.* She warmly acknowledges and respects her ghostwriter, who has been a tower of strength throughout this journey. This is her third book, and she extends her heartfelt gratitude to him. She is also deeply grateful to her bishop, Wayne Vernon, and her church family. As she continues her writing journey, Sophia remains forever humble.

www.ingramcontent.com/pod-product-compliance
Lightning Source LLC
Chambersburg PA
CBHW050000040726
47599CB00014B/1140